ACTING COMEDY

Despite being roundly cited as much harder to perform than its dramatic counterpart, comic acting is traditionally seen as a performance genre that can't be taught. At best it is often described as a skill that can only be learned "on the job" through years of practice, or given to a performer through natural talent.

Acting Comedy is an effort to examine this idea more rigorously by looking at different aspects of the comic actor's craft. Each chapter is written by an expert in a particular form—from actors and directors to teachers and stand-up comedians. Topics covered include:

- how performers work with audiences
- how comic texts can be enhanced through word and musical rhythm analysis
- how physical movements can generate comic moments and build character.

This book is an invaluable resource for any performer focusing on the minute details of comic acting, even down to *exactly* how one delivers a joke on stage. Christopher Olsen's unique collection of comic voices will prove essential reading for students and professionals alike.

Christopher Olsen began as an actor in the Off-Off Broadway theatre scene in New York City in the 1970s and 1980s and later received his PhD in Theatre History and Criticism from the University of Maryland. He continues to work as a Drama professor at the University of Puerto Rico.

ACTING COMEDY

Edited by Christopher Olsen

Routledge
Taylor & Francis Group

LONDON AND NEW YORK

First published 2016
by Routledge
2 Park Square, Milton Park, Abingdon, Oxon OX14 4RN

and by Routledge
711 Third Avenue, New York, NY 10017

Routledge is an imprint of the Taylor & Francis Group, an informa business

© 2016 Christopher Olsen

British Library Cataloguing-in-Publication Data
A catalogue record for this book is available from the British Library

Library of Congress Cataloguing-in-Publication Data
Olsen, Christopher, 1952–
Acting comedy / Christopher Olsen.
    pages cm
    1. Acting. 2. Comedy. I. Title.
    PN2071.C57O47 2015
    792.028–dc23   2015012710

ISBN: 978-1-138-89140-1 (hbk)
ISBN: 978-1-138-89141-8 (pbk)
ISBN: 978-1-315-70967-3 (ebk)

Typeset in Bembo
by HWA Text and Data Management, London

To all of our students

CONTENTS

FIGURES

CONTRIBUTORS

Candice Brown is a full-time faculty member of The Boston Conservatory, where she serves as the Coordinator for the Voice and Speech Division. Her teaching is in both the undergraduate and Master of Fine Arts Program. Her courses are in Voice and Speech and Acting in The Musical Theatre Division. Candice is a proud member of the Actors Equity Association, a Boston-based actor, as well as a professional vocal and dialect coach.

Judith Chaffee is Associate Professor Emerita at Boston University, where she headed Movement Training for Actors. A professional dancer, actor, choreographer, and director, her training and research have focused on movement modalities of physical comedy, *commedia dell'arte*, dance, improvisation, composition, Viewpoints, meditation, and devising theatre. She is co-editor with Olly Crick of the *Routledge Companion to Commedia dell'Arte*, and produced with Joel Asher two DVDs on period movement for Insight Media.

Merry Conway has developed her wit and wordplay work while teaching students at NYU, The Linklater Center, Shakespeare & Company, The Celebration Barn, and independent workshops in New York over the last several years. She has been involved with comedic forms since the 1970s. Merry received an NEA directing fellowship to study fool and clown in Shakespeare. For several years she was "The Clownmaster" at Shakespeare & Company, coaching the comic work. She worked as a theatrical clown, has done several seasons with Circus Flora, a one-ring circus with animals based in St. Louis, and also performed in New York with The Friendship Company, a group of mentally-challenged adults. She has taught at Carnegie Mellon University, and conducted numerous workshops and Master Classes for Emerson, Brandeis,

Cal Arts. She conducts workshops in Rome, Tuscania, Stromboli, and Calabria. She was an originating teacher at Shakespeare & Company. She has also taught in London at The Guildhall School, Mountview Theatre School and Drama Studio. www.merryconway.com

Greg Dean has been teaching and writing about the fundamentals of joke writing and performing stand-up comedy since 1982. When he began, Dean quickly realized there were no documented basics for teaching comedy. For the past three decades he's made it his life's mission to identify, name, and teach the basic techniques used by all great joke writers, comedians, and now actors. These fundamentals were first published in his paperback, eBook, and audio book *Step By Step to Stand-Up Comedy*. Dean lives with his wife, comedian/actress Gayla Johnson, in Los Angeles, CA. He's currently writing blogs with comedy tips and working on another book about comedy technique.

Steve Kaplan has been the industry's most sought-after expert on comedy for years. In addition to having taught at UCLA, NYU, Yale and other top universities, Steve Kaplan created the *HBO Workspace*, the *HBO New Writers Program* and was co-founder and Artistic Director of *Manhattan Punch Line Theatre*. He has served as a consultant to such companies as Dreamworks, Disney, HBO, Aardman Animation, and others. His new book, *The Hidden Tools of Comedy*, has been a best seller on Amazon.com and Kindle, and had been translated into Russian and Chinese. (I'm sure there's a joke in there, somewhere.) Steve has directed in regional theaters and Off-Broadway. He has been teaching his Comedy Intensive workshops around the world to thousands of students, with workshops scheduled in Los Angeles, New York, London, and Singapore.

Scott Meltzer, known as "Scotty" to his friend, has made a comfortable living as a comedy writer and comic juggler for over 30 years. His company, Comedy Industries, creates and performs customized comedy presentations for trade shows, sales meetings, training sessions, and other corporate events.

Christopher Olsen began as an actor in the Off-Off Broadway theatre scene in New York City in the 1970s and 1980s, and later received his PhD in Theatre History and Criticism from the University of Maryland. He continues to work as a Drama professor at the University of Puerto Rico, where he co-founded the "Bilingual Theatre Project," and where he continues to direct and write.

Davis Rider Robinson is founder and artistic director of the Beau Jest Moving Theater and professor of theater at Bowdoin College in Brunswick, Maine. He is author of *The Physical Comedy Handbook* and *A Practical Guide To Ensemble Devising*. He studied in Paris with Jacques Lecoq and in the United States with Tony Montanaro at the Celebration Barn Theater, where he teaches ensemble devising, improvisation, and physical comedy every summer.

Ian Wilkie is a life-long student of comedy. As Ian Angus Wilkie he still works from time to time as a comic actor in theatre and television. His PhD was on comic acting. He currently works at the UCL Institute of Education and is a visiting lecturer at the Guildhall in London. He is a member of TAPRA's popular performance advisory group and is a co-convener of *The London Comedy Forum*. He is articles editor for *Comedy Studies* and has written on comedy in adult-child interaction, art, teaching, Scottish humor and on curriculum review in actor training.

Shad Willingham is a professor of acting with the California State University, Northridge. Some directing credits: *Avenue Q, Romeo and Juliet, and The Servant of Two Masters* and *Twelfth Night* for the New Orleans Shakespeare Festival. Most recently playing Freddie in *Noises Off* for the Idaho Shakespeare Festival, Bottom in *A Midsummer Night's Dream* for the Lake Tahoe Shakespeare Festival and Marc Antony in *Antony and Cleopatra* for the Kingsmen Shakespeare Festival. After receiving his Masters of Fine Arts Degree from the University of Washington in 2002, Shad joined the acting company of the Oregon Shakespeare Festival for six seasons performing in over a dozen productions. Shad is also a graduate of the North Carolina School of the Arts, the British American Drama Academy, the Moscow Art Theatre training program and the United Stuntman's Association. He is a member of Actors Equity Association, Screen Actors Guild and the Stage Directors and Choreographers Society. Shad is married to Heidi Dippold and they a have a beautiful daughter named Tess.

INTRODUCTION

Christopher Olsen

I thought about opening the introduction with a list of thoughtful quotations about comedy from famous practitioners and thinkers of the present and the past, but as I perused the Internet I realized there are thousands and thousands of quips and anecdotes about the application of comedy. It would take months just to read and decipher all of them. So I thought "Why not begin with how and why our book came to be, and what we all hope to achieve with this collective work from comedy teachers and practitioners?"

I would like you for a minute to imagine being in the mind of a young, insecure, 21-year-old actor who is faced with the prospect of participating in a three-hour improvisation class in which most of the scenes will end up being comic in nature. The class is made up of about 25 young acting students and among them are the "natural" comic actors who seem to move effortlessly from one improv to another generating laughs and creating funny business. For him, who neither saw himself as particularly funny on stage nor had the courage to break out from his "safe" shell to explore humor, this class was excruciating. It reminded him of sitting in a party and everybody telling jokes and funny stories to the others but when it came to his turn to tell a story the members of the party would politely smile as he laboriously told his funny story—and then they would quickly change the subject. Of course, that 21-year-old was me.

Acting conservatories tend to stress the truthfulness and honesty of bringing a character to life on stage. "Stay in the moment" and don't *do* anything unless someone causes you to do it. "Acting is reacting," and, for God's sakes, "stop acting." The Stanislavski approach (and its descendants and offshoots) is a serious business and requires years and years of training, application, and simple maturity as an actor. For the most part you are working in the realm of realism and performing in plays that have a fourth wall and require you to be believable and convincing as the character you are portraying. The more depth, range, and innovation you invest your character with, the more you are appreciated for your professionalism. Actors who win Tony Awards and Oscars often are rewarded as "good actors" because they can play a variety of serious roles in great plays and films. Sometimes they win for comic roles but that is rare. When is the last time you remember anyone winning an Oscar for a comic role? I can—he is Italian and his name is Roberto Benigni, who won an Oscar for a film called *Life is Beautiful* in 1998. And that was a particularly dark comic film.

To create comedy is a most difficult activity because it requires such concentration, rhythmic sensitivity, the ability to work with others, and the courage of a space explorer. It requires even more concentration on stage than playing a dramatic role because you have three entities to engage with—yourself operating within the character, your fellow characters you are interacting with on stage, and the audience in the seats. Every performance requires you to interact with all three and if any part of that triad alters during a performance, the effect can be colossal. Why do so many actors say that matinees feel so different from evening performances because of the change in the character of the audiences? Cultural differences concerning the relationships between audience and performers can also alter the theatre experience—especially as it pertains to comedy. There are considerations of the socio-economic status between audience members and stage performers. In commercial theatre in Europe and in the US by and large we still observe the Victorian tradition of proscenium staging with a well-mannered audience applauding politely at the end of a production after the approximately two-hour "trafficking" across the stage. A well-known comic actor may receive a different reception from a totally unknown one even if they are playing the same role. But, as most good actors know, no matter where you perform and to whom you perform in front of—whether it is stand-up comedy in a small club or a sit-down drawing room comedy in a Broadway theatre, the razor-sharp line between success and failure, between laughter and silence, between good taste and vulgarity; between shock and boredom, continues every night of a performance.

If this book is a potpourri of comedy instruction, it provides the reader with a wide range of smells and flavors. I sought contributors from a variety of backgrounds and who teach/perform in a variety of areas of comedy. Many of the contributors have already written books on their own but I was able to convince them that the purpose of this volume was to provide actors and performers with a comprehensive "acting text" for different types of comedy. It would contain anecdotes and comic exercises from different voices and become a kind of Stanislavskian acting guide—not "An Actor Prepares," but perhaps "A Comic Actor Prepares." I asked the contributors to visualise their chapter as an acting class focusing on a topic or two. They were free to suggest any topic and as long we didn't have exact repetitions they were free to indulge in whatever they chose. As it turned out, without knowing each other's topics, several of the writers overlapped in giving identical examples which, of course, is fine because one area of comedy can easily evoke another and vice versa. I realized that the book could not cover comedy in a comprehensive global context, but the writers have all drawn from their backgrounds (primarily British/American) and made references with a more global reading audience in mind. Charlie Chaplin's comedy certainly doesn't need to be "translated" for a wider, global audience.

In Chapter 1, Ian Wilkie explores audience interplay as a defining feature of comic acting. Dramatic truth and comic truth are different concepts and require alternative routes and different acting approaches by the performer. In Chapter 2, Steve Kaplan explains how comedy is created by someone struggling to make sense of things versus someone else who is blind to his/hers predicament. He calls the conflict "the Wavy Line versus the Straight Line," and suggests that when acting the Straight Line the focus should be on either creating obstacles for the Wavy Line or being indifferent to the obstacles that are there whereas playing a Wavy Line moment requires a vulnerability and cluelessness about making sense of a seemingly hopeless predicament. In Chapter 3, Candice Brown considers the importance of understanding punctuation when developing comic timing within lines. Brown focuses on the playwright George Bernard Shaw, and creates what she calls Intrinsic Shavian Cadence (ISC) as a reliable technique for bringing out the musicality of Shavian wit. In Chapter 4, Judith Chaffee brings her expertise in *commedia dell'arte* to the forefront and reveals how the characters of *commedia* must be reflective of archetypes in societies throughout the world. She introduces the main tenants of *commedia* but also shows how its comic traditions inform modern comic business—and how the traditional "Lazzis" can be used in more modern stage settings. In Chapter 5, Davis Rider Robinson focuses specifically on acting in farces. He emphasizes that even though farce seems chaotic, messy, and uncontrollable, the reality is good farcical acting requires a kind of musicality in the actors and a deep attention to each other's movements and utterances. Good farce must "float" and not be "flattened." In Chapter 6, Christopher Olsen uses a well-known movement technique to facilitate collective rehearsals called "Viewpoints" in exploring gestures in comedy. Gestures have become so intrinsic to comic acting but can be created from different paradigms and used to produce moments that provide the basis for so many comic scenes on stage. In Chapter 7, Merry Conway develops a working method to approach comic texts from other historical eras by rekindling the childhood fun in playing with language. Using puns, limericks, and story-telling techniques, she asks actors to develop their abilities in manipulating language and finding new avenues for generating wit and word repartee. In Chapter 8, Greg Dean focuses on the structure of jokes and explains how jokes are based on two vital parts—setup and punch. He goes on to provide numerous examples of how a joke can be manipulated and honed as long as the comic actor observes the main necessary ingredients for success. In Chapter 9, Scott Meltzer puts one in the mind of a stand-up comedian and explains how to use timing, audience manipulation, and verbal dexterity to create a desired result on stage. Using the term "Comic Darwinism," Meltzer writes that you need two things: random mutation and natural selection. Finally, in Chapter 10,

Shad Willingham provides "5½ rules" for developing better improvisation skills that will enhance your comic performing. He includes such useful approaches as "fail big," using irony, and learning how to "fake" things until the interplay becomes more organic among your fellow improvisers.

To end this introduction, I have had second thoughts about using a few quotations about comedy that I mentioned in the beginning. I want to address just four of them briefly, as they relate to our book. Here they are:

> I want to write a book which is the history of comedy.
>
> John Cleese

> You can't study comedy; it's within you. It's a personality. My humor is an attitude.
>
> Don Rickles

> The secret to humor is surprise.
>
> Aristotle

> When I'm good, I'm very good, but when I'm bad, I'm better.
> Mae West to Cary Grant in *I'm no Angel*

Well, to John, we say we hope you do it but in the meantime we are giving you some historical anecdotes about comic acting down through the ages in this book. To Don, we politely disagree because we are proving that you can indeed study comedy. You got to be so good, Don, because you spent so many years practicing your comedy in front of audiences. To Ari, we can only agree as all of us laud the unpredictable comic actor who can come up with original business no matter in what situation she/he is in. And, finally, to Mae West—we all hope that our book will inspire more "bad" comic acting.

1

'THROUGH WALL'S CHINK'

Or, audience interplay in comic acting

Ian Wilkie

> And through Wall's chink (poor souls) they are content
> To Whisper
>
> > (Peter Quince's Prologue in Shakespeare's
> > *A Midsummer Night's Dream*, act 5, scene 1)

Interplay, the fourth wall and 'truth' in comic acting

All forms of live performance require the establishment of some kind of interplay between the performer and audience. The presentation of a theatrical event requires the making of a 'contract' (Verma in Giannachi and Luckhurst 1999: 129) wherein performers and audience enter into a specialised form of intercommunication. Live performance, as a system of communication, requires each party to play their pre-established and ongoing role within the pretence; to suspend disbelief for the duration of the action; and to respond in particular ways to the event's action as it unfolds. As Aston and Savona note in *Theatre as Sign-System*, 'the spectator … is engaged in a project of creative collaboration with the dramatist and actor in the interest of a more complete realisation of the performance' (1991: 160).

During the performance, moreover, the actor will, consciously or unconsciously, gauge the effectiveness of her/his performance through the establishment of a form of interplay with the audience and may respond in consequence to the feedback received by altering the performance. The actor responds to the audience's reception to the performance, even, arguably, through listening for, hearing and evaluating the different 'quality' of any silences that may be received during the event and, possibly, correspondingly, adapting what she/he is doing in response. The actor, Michael Pennington refers, apropos of performing as Hamlet, to, 'the actor's third ear, by which he monitors as far as he can, the nature of the silence in the house on a particular night' (in Brockbank 1988: 128). Audience signals that the actor may receive might be overt and auditory, taking, for example, the form of laughter, murmurs, sighs, disapprobatory utterances, intense silences and, perhaps, even applause, all made in direct response to the performance. In this way, live performance is reliant on connections made with an audience and the spectators' making of reciprocal communicative responses to the action.

Theatre practitioners and theorists alike have referred in different ways to this direct interplay between actor and audience as being crucial to the act of live performance. *Theatre de Complicité* director Simon McBurney states that 'audience and the acknowledgment of the audience are fundamental to me: there has to be that thread of companionship' (in Giannachi and Luckhurst 1999: 73). Russian director and theorist Vsevolod Meyerhold, meanwhile, referred to the spectator as the 'fourth creator' (in Thomson 2000: 174) while Peter Brook notes 'the true function of the spectator, there and not there, ignored and yet needed. The actors work is never for an audience, yet always is for one … this implies a sharing of experience, once contact is made' (1968: 57).

In comedy and comic acting, 'the reactions evoked in an audience' (Biner 1972: 168) contain particularly profound significance in shaping and deciding the effectiveness of the form of creative expression itself. For comic actors, the audience's laughter provides an instantly measureable phenomenon. Audience responsiveness, moreover, can directly affect what performers do in performance and in a live comedy event actors will tend to respond, in turn, to the audience's instant feedback through their laughter. Freud remarked that, 'the comic is content with only two persons, one who finds the comical, and one in whom it is found' ([1905] 1964: 70) and McIlvenny et al. note that the spectators' laughter response to the actors' performance 'is the only immediate way in which a performer can test, gauge and establish audience approval' (1993: 230). In this singular way, interplay in comic acting can be seen, at its most basic level, as the inevitability of the actor in a comedy listening to the audience's response and adjusting the performance accordingly – even by merely lengthening or shortening the pause which allows the laughter to peak, variously, and in response to each and every performance circumstance. Even though 'that "acknowledgment" constitutes no "acknowledgment"' (Gruber 1986: 132) and in situations where the comic actor has to work 'within the representational frame [that] demands that the actors always be "in character"' (ibid.), still, as Glasgow notes, 'the metatheatrical aspect of comedy … links actor and audience … even if the linkage is normally now internalised or banished into the thematic innards of … [a] … play' (1995: 137).

Audience interplay, then, is a defining feature of comic acting and one which in the performer's responsiveness to laughter differentiates comic acting from non-comic forms. As John Wright wryly notes, albeit writing more specifically of physical comedy, 'you're not doing comedy if nobody laughs' (2007: 5).

In the modern age, for comic actors working in the Anglo-American tradition, the notion of establishing direct interplay between performer and audience has become complicated and contentious. This is for two main reasons, both of which are rooted in the tendency for the pursuit of 'naturalism' or 'realism' that predominates in widely accepted forms of modern theatre. The first of these limiting factors for the comic actor's use of interplay is due to the convention of the 'fourth wall':

> *Soit donc que vous composiez, soit que vous jouiez, ne pensez non plus au spectateur que s'il n'existait pas. Imaginez, sur le bord du théâtre, un grand mur qui vous sépare du parterre: jouez comme si la toile ne se levait pas.*

> [Imagine a huge wall across the front of the stage, separating you from the audience, and behave exactly as if the curtain had never risen]
>
> (Diderot 1758)

In earlier theatrical formulations to Diderot's, undisguised interplay was an accepted formulation of performance, particularly in comic forms, from ritual and early Greek drama onwards. Although, as William Gruber notes, 'direct address did not exist in early tragedy' (1986: 16) audience address characterised the early comic form. The actors would directly address the audience in Aristophanes' fifth-century BC comedies:

> Drawing it into the action, now flattering it grossly, now abusing it with tongue in cheek … In return the audience didn't just laugh but applauded, hissed, booed, drummed the wooden benches with their heels, or called out as the fancy took them.
>
> (Cartledge 1999: 9)

The presence of the (proto-stand-up) figure of the comic interlocutor character was also commonly to be found in post-classical comic drama. In assuming the role of a subversive trickster figure or anti-hero idler (Ritchie 2006) the comic interlocutor would directly address the audience and in this way, incite collaboration in order to get the spectators 'on-side'. Such comic interlocutors, or 'licensed fool' roles, are still evident in many non-western forms of drama, such as the 'bhand' of Pakistan (Emigh and Emigh 1986) or the 'puson' in the Philippines (Bayliss et al. 2004).

From medieval times, in Europe, the gradual formalisation of the work of disparate groups of itinerant players that evolved into the recognisable, professional, modern, theatrical tradition saw the comedian continuing his role as direct commentator on social mores. In the direct address formulations of Elizabethan theatre, for example, the audience interplay skills of the comic performer were paramount and were given a rare prominence by the playwrights. Shakespeare, for example, created parts to highlight the skills of his comic players. John Russell Brown cites the examples of Sincklo, Cowley and Kemp being specifically mentioned by Shakespeare in his original play texts and notes that 'none of the straight actors of the company ever crept into the stage directions in the same way' (1993: 87). In the seventeenth century, Restoration comedy demanded interplay between the comic performer and the audience. As Simon Callow notes in Acting in Restoration Comedy, 'the plays … demand a special complicity between the actor and audience' (1991: 12).

However, it was with the rise of naturalism in the nineteenth century and the growing pre-eminence of role of the director and playwright in dramatic formulation, that the performer's creative input and her/his practice of comic interplay skills and license to engage directly with the audience became increasingly compromised. By the late nineteenth century, the conceptual fourth wall was firmly in place in theatre, disastrously hampering comic actors' ability to engage in any direct interplay with the audience. The establishment of the fourth wall would henceforth affect actors' ability to fashion a type of comic performance which, as actor and comedian Stephen Fry describes it, directly 'allow[s] an audience in' (2010: 108).

The second feature, connected with the rise of 'naturalism' which has limited comic actors' development of interplay was due to what John Wright terms 'the pervasive legacy of Stanislavski' (2007: xiv). Modern Anglo-American performance styles owe much to the teachings of the influential Russian theorist, actor and director, Constantin Stanislavski (1863–1938). Stanislavski wrote of the creation of what he termed 'scenic truth' ([1936] 1986: 128), realised through the actor's use of 'imagination [which] plays, by far, the greatest part' in helping to 'constitute "art" on stage' (*ibid.*). The Stanislavski system's terminologies of 'super-objective, logic of actions, given circumstances, communion, subtext, images, tempo-rhythm' (Moore 1974: 9), have subsequently become the accepted rubric of westernised performance. The modern actor's role in the theatre-making process is to present 'a character [as] a new human being, born of the elements of the actor himself united with those of the character conceived by the playwright' (*ibid.*: 17) where 'it is the truth of the actor's behaviour that will keep the audience's attention' (*ibid.*: 18).

In essence, however, the often 'unacknowledged presence … of Stanislavski' (Brockbank 1988: 5) means that the modern actor is expected to follow a method of theatre making which emphasises the depiction of 'truth' or behavioural 'realisms' that the audience can recognise as authentic. Dramatic representations of human action are arrived at through a process of inner exploration of motivations and by the actor following internalised, broadly psychoanalytical routes in order to discover 'truthful' solutions. As John Miles-Brown notes, 'Stanislavski required actors to … develop powers of imagination … to believe in the characters within the stage situation; to work from conscious techniques in order to liberate subconscious reactions (the psycho-technique)' (2000: 12).

Stanislavski's pathway to the presentation of such 'realistic' depictions of human psychological behaviour has become the accepted *sine qua non* of western performance culture. However, dramatic 'truth' and comic 'truth' are rather different entities and each requires the pursuit of alternative routes and the employment of different acting approaches by the performer. Any dichotomy between comic and non-comic truth is not always recognised in the teaching, learning and practice of theatre and drama, even though the quasi-representational worlds that are presented in each form are, usually, radically different. The overall text in comic drama usually depends on heightened, quirky or off-kilter premises that usually end in happy resolution and that are designed to elicit amusement and, ideally, to allow audience laughter. The worlds presented in non-comic texts are essentially depictions of humans in conflict and are, conversely, not predominantly designed to elicit or allow audience laughter. In essence, the stakes in comic drama tend to be different and less serious. These differentiated forms of manufactured fiction, therefore, must rely on different representations of 'truth' within their contingent contexts. Comic 'truth' differs from dramatic 'truth' in quite fundamental ways and requires extra layers for the comic actor to add in rehearsal in creating a character on top of any Stanislavskian solutions that may be achieved in the process.

In *The Craft of Comedy* – a rare and reflective meditation on the subject from the actor's perspective by the actress Athene Seyler, originally written in 1943 – Seyler characterises comedy as being based on a 'distorted truth' (1990: 2), one that depends on the performer employing 'the craft of appearing to believe in the balance of a thing one knows is out of balance' (*ibid*.: 12). Such 'balance' is, arguably, even more difficult for the actor to achieve in comedy where the fiction is often more prescriptive (i.e. often operating with more obviously stereotypical characters than in tragedy; using a preponderance of stock situations and plots; employing more arbitrary and implausible coincidences that are independent of overtly external or internal fatalistic flaws, or the dictates of inevitability; and through the preference for the resolution of happy endings.

Nonetheless, within a less 'realistic', more contrived comic world, comic acting must still, somehow, be recognisably 'true' within the modern performance idiom. As comic actors themselves note 'comedy must be founded on truth and on an understanding of the real value of a character before it can pick out the highlights' (Seyler 1990: 5); 'everything must spring from truth' (Constant Coquelin 1954: 66) and 'the basis of any technique must be "Truth"' (Maggie Smith in O'Brien 1983: 204). As the actress Margaret Rutherford wrote of playing Madame Arcati in Blithe Spirit:

> Underneath the comic façade I saw a real person of flesh and blood with serious beliefs. I never intend to be a satirist, I never intend to play for laughs. I am always surprised that audiences think me funny at all. I find it hard to analyse what I do except perhaps in my timing. And for this I am grateful to Marie Tempest who taught me everything I know in the all important control of laughter. If my work looks effortless, it is not. It is a question of tireless polishing the whole time. For this very reason I played Madame Arcati straight and real.
>
> (Rutherford 1972: 47)

In essence, as the comic improvisers Charna Halpern and Del Close maintain, 'the truth is funny' (2001: 15). Comic truth and reality, however, start from a fundamentally different premise and stem from different roots than that of non-comic theatre forms. The essence of comedy – indeed, one of the major 'principles' of comedy – is that of 'incongruity' (Double 1997: 89; Provine 2000: 12–18; Raskin 1985: 30–41) in which 'the familiar as if it were strange' applies (Morreall 1987: 2). Incongruity in comedy:

> Does not match up with what we expect things of that kind to be, or because it is out of place in the setting in which we find it. Something amuses us if it somehow violates our picture of the way things are supposed to be, and if we enjoy this violation
>
> (Morreall 1987: 216)

Arthur Schopenhauer, meanwhile, famously defined the operation of incongruity in comedy as:

> The phenomenon of laughter always signifies the sudden apprehension of an incongruity between such a conception and the real object thought under it ... the greater and more unexpected, in the apprehension of the laugher, this incongruity is, the more violent will be his laughter
>
> (Schopenhauer 1907: 54–55)

Oddness or 'violation' of expectation is, then, perhaps, the most ubiquitous form of comic creativity. It is the recognition of a surprising juxtaposition of what is right with what is wrong that strikes us as being funny. Comic theatre, then, represents a case of an already fictionalised dramatic reality (the theatrical event) being subjected to a further twist (i.e. the addition of the comically incongruous elements). The comic actor has to juggle her/his representation of truth and reality within an alternatively fictionalised, 'funnier' dramatic context. The actor must find appropriate levels of reaction to incongruous circumstances in comic theatre. In performance terms, the operation of incongruity (Seyler's playing of a 'distorted truth') may be most obvious in the work of the clown. The clown is a highly stylised figure who subverts normality e.g. through her/his depiction of failure to complete a simple task; through the presentation of a series of minor and unlikely catastrophes; and the creation of a sense of mayhem, all intended for comic effect. Incongruity is also overtly evident in some comedians' costume choices (and televisual or film images might include Harry Hill's overlarge shirt collar, Norman Wisdom's fore-shortened suit or any item from Phyllis Diller's wardrobe). Incongruity may be physically manifest in comedians' movement (and, again, filmic representations of extreme bodily examples might include Max Wall's eccentric dancing (i.e. a mournful, dignified man moving on rubbery, expressive legs); or in John Cleese's absurdist movements around the 'Ministry of Silly Walks' in *Monty Python's Flying Circus* (BBC, 1969–74).

It must, however, be acknowledged that comic acting theorists do not disavow the notion of 'truthful' playing in the making of comic theatre. Seyler, for example, identifies Stanislavskian 'subtextual' factors as being crucial to the execution of comic performance:

> In playing comedy I am sure one has to rely first on the subconscious or inspirational method of reading a part by sinking oneself in the character, and then check the results consciously from outside oneself and keep what seems good, and discard what is overdone or what misses fire. It's a kind of dual control of one's performance.
>
> (Seyler 1990: 52)

In her text *Style: Acting in High Comedy*, the actress Maria Aitken highlights the intermediary role of the performer, describing comedians as 'the middlemen: the actors who have to catch the comic spark from the playwright and pass it on to the audience' (1996: 4) while also acknowledging the need for finding 'truth' – 'the words demand display as well as truthfulness' (*ibid.*: 5). She too, emphasises the necessity for the actor to maintain a 'dual control' of focus on the performance – 'we actors experience simultaneous connection and disconnection with our character. Comedy requires a parallel universe' (*ibid.*: 9).

Nor, in all fairness, do Stanislavskians totally disavow the notion of interplay in modern theatre making. Lee Strasberg, the father of 'method' acting, describes the performer's role in this intercommunicative process as:

> On stage the actor ... must be ninety nine per cent actor and a little bit critic and a little bit audience ... acting is a profession where the doing and the awareness of doing go hand in hand – and not after the doing but during the moment of doing.
>
> (Strasberg in Hethmon 1966: 84)

The process of depicting comic truth however, is not made entirely explicit for comic actors by the influential acting theorists. Practitioners themselves seem to accept that some species of truth needs to be presented. The actor John Gielgud maintained that the actor 'may sometimes find a different kind of truth ... a solemn yet light kind for farce' (1965: 8). John Wright states that 'the strongest comedy comes from the greatest seriousness' (2007: 326) while Halpern and Close note that 'the more ridiculous the situation, the more seriously it must be played ... the actors must be totally committed to their characters and play them with complete integrity to achieve maximum laughs' (2001: 25). Theorist Henri Bergson offered a definition of the operation of truth in comedy in the following terms – 'when a certain comic effect has its origin in a certain cause, the more natural we regard the cause to be, the more comic shall we find the effect' ([1900] 1994: 122). Undoubtedly, however, this weaving and sustaining of a comic truth, however it may be defined – and whether achieved as an individual or as part of an ensemble – is a very tricky enterprise for the comic actor; in Seyler's terms it is a form of 'tightrope walking' (1990: 12).

In comic performance, then, audience interplay, or the 'link' made between actor and audience, is a key factor, both in the interchange that the laughter response sets up and even in the way in which, for example, the 'expectation of pleasurable performance – the workings of the comic and humour – rather than narrative suspense are currencies of audience exchange' (Mellencamp 1986: 91). Furthermore, the maintaining of comic truth within a form of theatre where interplay must still pertain produces conditions that are particularly tricky for the comic actor to negotiate. The contradictory polarities that the comic actor must master during live performance make comic acting a particularly complicated, specialised and skilful form of theatrical representation, in as much as 'acting becomes more complex as more elements are incorporated into the pretence' (Kirby 1987: 20). Given, then, the dictates of modern theatre generally, that is, the limitations enforced by the fourth wall, the comic actor's own strict framing within the dramatic event and the negotiation of the formula of distorted 'truth' that comic theatre presents, how, then does interplay operate in practice in comic acting?

Interplay in comic acting

As the playwright Friedrich Durrenmatt noted, 'the audience of a comedy is a reality to be counted upon' (1964: 268) and acting in a live comedy is dependent on, and affected by, an audience in a way that other forms of performance are not. Comic acting requires both direct attention and responsiveness to an audience's response. Audience laughter automatically means that interaction and reaction is occurring in the live performance event and, clearly, if there is no laughing, there can be no comedy. As the American comedian and director Mike Nichols noted of stand-up comedians, 'comedy is the only work in the world in which the work and the reward are simultaneous. Comedians get it on the spot. They get the laugh' (Lahr 2001: 274).

The audience's response, then, is a vital, defining feature of comic performance and the comic actor's role includes the establishment of interplay in recognising and adapting to that response. As Andy Medhurst states, 'the core mission of all … comedy [is] the eliciting of complicity' (2003: 140) and part of the comic actor's job is to be attentive in order to keep the channels of complicit interplay between actor and audience open. In live performance, the interplay of comic message transmitted by the actor(s) and the received response from the audience occur both instantaneously and as part of an exponential process throughout the performance and it allows for mutual evaluation of the effectiveness of the theatrical event to be simultaneously and continuously undertaken. Recognition of the responsiveness of the audience forms a vital ingredient of the comic actor's repertoire of skills, and this interplay, means that, in a very real sense, 'the audience 'makes' the comedy' (Greig 1969: 221). Here 'an audience is both shaped by the talk it is attending' and through its responses 'help shape what will be made of that talk' (Goodwin 1986: 311). For the comic actor, 'interplay', then, describes not merely an awareness of, but a conscious interaction with, and responsiveness to, the audience. The mode of interplay can, of course, be entirely explicit (as in the case of the transmissions of the stand-up comic or clown) or, as in the case of the comic actor working within a play or theatricalised text, it may, of necessity, assume some of the more implicit forms mentioned above. Thus, as Brett Mills states 'performers respond to the ways in which audiences react to the comedy which is performed for them, and this is more than simply allowing them time to laugh' (2005: 89).

So even a simple pause to allow a laugh to punctuate the performance signals that acting in a comedy requires an, albeit tacit, acknowledgement of the audience's responsiveness. This unacknowledged 'acknowledgement' of a response, cued by an audience's laughter, in turn, can affect the actor's playing of a moment, her/his holding of a pause, emphasising of a look or stressing of a word or line. Conversely, the audience can feel cheated by the performer who barrels through the laugh or who 'kills' the comic moment by failing to hear how the audience's responsive cues are attempting to prompt and affect her/his performance. In such instances of inattentiveness by the comic actor the interplay link is temporarily destroyed. As Susan Purdie notes, 'when we laugh at performed events, we really know that a Teller is both inciting and receiving our transgressive response' (1993: 16) and an audience can feel cheated if their role in the making of the comic meaning is thwarted. To this extent, interplay between the audience and the comic actors also relies on the (tacit) acknowledgement that both parties are willing to engage in a suspension of truth and are adopting a more 'playful' state – that is, each accepting that they enter into a contract to participate in a game (the comic play) which requires its own unique set of rules to be obeyed by each of the sides involved. The state of mutually playful engagement allows the conditions for the interplay in the comic game to proceed and both actor and audience need equal awareness of the rules of engagement for the complete comic flow to be able to occur. An audience who refuses to participate openly in the comic game through responsively sharing their laughter are often characterised by performers as 'bad' or 'quiet'.

Yet how might comic actors achieve interplay in situations where no direct interplay is possible, that is, in productions where the inhibiting fourth wall is required to be in place? Athene Seyler describes it thus:

> When I talk of establishing direct contact with the audience I mean a subtle psychological bond, perhaps merely the subconscious acknowledgement that your job as a comedian is to point out something to the audience, and that the audience's reaction to this makes up an integral part of your job.
>
> (Seyler 1990: 4)

More technically, the Edwardian comic actor, George Graves describes the building of audience interplay in his autobiography:

> In my own job I have learnt more by far from the audience than from any other source. In a way the comic's task is something like that of the author, for our actual past is usually a framework in which we build up our performance. And however satisfied I am at rehearsals with a joke, a bit of business or a situation, I have always tried to gather the reaction of the audience to it and to refashion my show in accordance with the public response.
>
> (Graves 1931: 148–149)

A concrete example of the comic actor responding in turn to an audience's response, engaging in interplay and subverting the fourth wall within a play can be found in Martin Jarvis's published production diary of By Jeeves (Lloyd Webber and Ayckbourn 1996):

> I may have found a new laugh. It's quite a good moment – after Bertie's 'Do you think that they're following it, this lot?' Intriguing how a tiny move can make all the difference: instead of having my eyes already fixed upon the house, I shifted my gaze crisply from John towards the audience as if to evaluate their intelligence. Big laugh. Then a firmer second laugh, as Jeeves decides, 'impossible to tell, sir'.
>
> (Jarvis 2003: 213)

However, in his book Liveness, Philip Auslander claims that 'the "energy" that supposedly exists between performers and spectators in a live event' (2008: 2–3) is a 'cliché and a mystification' (*ibid.*), while conceding that 'concepts such as these do have value for performers … Indeed it may be necessary for performers … to believe in them' (*ibid.*). This is, surely, a misreading of what actually occurs in live performance, evaluated from a non-practitioner's perspective. To deny that awareness between performers and audience exists and to suggest that there is no intercommunicative exchange of 'energy' between them is an attempt to apply too rigidly empiricist a set of analytical requirements. While, admittedly, it may be difficult to find the words to express what actually occurs in such performer/receiver exchanges, this does not mean that such intercommunicative exchanges do not exist. Indeed, the connective flow between performer and audience in a live situation can easily be interrupted and disturbed by something as trivial as, say, the wrong sort of cough in a violin recital (Bryant 2014: 9) or a mobile phone going off in mid-performance (BBC 2005). Interplay, therefore, in the sense of the 'energy' between actor and audience being mutually assessed in live performance situations is a very real phenomenon.

Interplay features specifically in comic acting in various ways, George Graves talks of 'trying to sense the audience's mood' (*ibid.*: 184) and comedian and actor Stephen Fry refers to the operation of interplay as:

The almost hyperaesthetical way in which one was aware of each microsecond on stage, of how one could detect precisely where an audience's focus was at any time, I loved the thrill of knowing that I was carrying hundreds of people with me.

(Fry 2010: 109)

Comedian Bob Monkhouse would suggest, indeed, that audience interplay is what designates great comedy, as epitomised in 'the art of the best comedians – elevating the material by the implication of an unspoken understanding between themselves and the audience' (1998: 195).

What may well be true, however, is that responding to the audience's cues can, conversely, lead the comic actor down false routes and into performing what the US comedian Phil Silvers termed 'hokum' (1973: 26–7), meaning cod performative commonalities that exist only in hackneyed comic acting. The actor Michael Redgrave described the danger inherent in relying too much on, or misreading, the cues received by the actor in performer/spectator interplay: 'It is a fallacy to believe that the audience is ipso facto of assistance to the actor. It can force him to dominate their mood … with force or tricks which are alien to the part he is playing' (1995: 37). Or, as the comic Dickie Henderson expressed it, 'the biggest trap you can fall into is listening to the audience's reaction instead of the other actors on the stage' (in Cotes 1989: 56).

On purely practical grounds though, for the comic actor, the monitoring of the volume and quality of laughter does provide an instantaneous, reflective, evaluation on practice that is a much more reliable indicator of the effectiveness of the performance than, arguably, the perception of a 'silent' response is for practitioners working in non-comic forms. In comedy, the audience's contract means that they enter into a kind of complicity with the performer in which laughter becomes both the objective and the mutual reward. The building of complicity seems essential for the comic acting in live performance.

Comic acting in film and television, however, requires a different, more muted and less open style, and the establishment of interplay and complicity are doubly problematic for comic actors to achieve when working within these media, or, as William Cook expresses the problem for comic performers in Ha Bloody Ha: Comedians Talking, 'when the fourth wall that [comedians] strive so hard to pull down is replaced by an invisible, bullet-proof glass panel' (1994: 249). In television comedy, particularly in sitcom, the presence of a studio audience is, accordingly, common practice, in order to recreate an impression of immediacy, communality and rapport for the home viewer. Otherwise, to recreate the sense of interplay, as Carr and Greeves note, an artificial solution is still used – 'TV comedy without a studio audience is … problematic. [Consequently,] a CBS executive, named Charlie Douglass, invented canned laughter' (2007: 118).

It is, therefore, fascinating to note how often comedians and comic actors working in film and television, do break through and defy the convention of the fourth wall by directly addressing the audience down the camera lens. In the

US, comedians such as Oliver Hardy, Groucho Marx and Bob Hope all directly addressed the audience in their films, while in the UK, ex-music hall performers such as George Formby (a 'top box-office draw of the late thirties', according to Halliwell 1987: 309) ensured interplay through direct address to camera. John Fisher, for example, refers to Formby's 'likeability' (1975: 8), 'warmth' (*ibid*.: 19), 'familiarity' (*ibid*.: 21), 'rapport' (*ibid*.: 89) and 'the sense of complicity of all great comedians' (*ibid*.: 87).

Similarly, popular British comedians on television often defied the fourth wall and used direct address to camera to connect with the home audience from whom they felt disabled and detached. The actor Nigel Hawthorne refers to Frankie Howerd's 'stepping out of the frame' (Hawthorne 2002: 128), while Eric Morecambe perfected mid-action cut-away looks and broad grins to the camera in his work. Contemporaneously, writer/performer Miranda Hart stated, 'I want to do looks to camera. I want a studio audience. And I want each episode to end with a musical number' (in Walker 2011: 12). Ricky Gervais, meanwhile, has used direct address to the camera to more subversive and satirical ends – as a means to character revelation – in his portrayal of would-be comedian David Brent in The Office (BBC, 2001–3).

An instance of how comic actors have an awareness of the need for a duality of approach in performing for the live studio audience and for the home audience is evident in an example taken from comic actor Ronnie Barker's account of the making of The Two Ronnies (BBC, 1971–87). This TV sketch and character monologue show featured Barker and fellow comic actor Ronnie Corbett, and the former explains how they differentiated their playing between the present, live audience and the audience at home. First, 'we did everything to keep the audience warm – you'd pull silly faces, shove your glasses up your nose, anything, right up to the opening word of the next sketch' (Barker 1988: 114). Then, Barker describes the need to maintain a concomitant level of audience awareness for the filmed inserts when no studio audience was present during recording to 'help shape' the comedy through their response:

> Ronnie C and I used to psych each other up during filming for The Two Ronnies; you had to be about twenty per cent higher to make up for having no audience, 'Energy, energy, energy' we'd tell each other, just before each take.
>
> (Barker 1988: 120)

In essence, the comic actor needs the response to evaluate how her/his acting is working. The actor's reaction to the audience's response is, in itself, a necessary violation of the fourth wall and comic actors will often aspire to establish interplay with their audience by playing with, or subverting, the convention of the fourth wall. This 'stepping out of the frame' demarcates many other types of more overtly performative comic modes, such as stand-up or clowning, where, whenever possible, 'unlike an actor in a play, the comedian breaks through the fourth wall' (Carr and Greeves 2007: 113).

Notions of how comic actors negotiate the fourth wall lead to the question of how the actor can also present Stanislavskian 'truth' while still having awareness of, and engaging in interplay of any kind with the audience. Believability and truthfulness in comic acting must always still apply. Indeed, acceptable depictions of a kind of 'truth' in comic theatre remain vital to the activity. Believability must register with the audience, albeit that comic acting operates within a world of heightened truth. Comic truth in performance is a highly manufactured and negotiated state, arising, as it does from a mutually accepted suspension of disbelief and managing to be sustained within and throughout a series of circumstantial fictions. Despite this, comic truth remains a relatively instantly recognisable condition, accepted and endorsed by the audience if it is played well by the comic actors. The actor's skills are in her/his seemingly authentic presentation of inauthenticity. As comic actor Nicholas Parsons notes, 'the essential element of truth in a ... comedy situation has to exist, or the audience will stop laughing' (1994: 146).

Ultimately, any sense of 'comic truth' is valid only if it registers as 'true' by the audience. An audience is able immediately to detect and reject as 'phoney' or 'untrue' any interaction or piece of 'business' that seem faked. Comic performance is, regrettably, often full of such false signals which only serve to disestablish the sense of comic truth. Examples of what Phil Silvers termed 'hokum', as mentioned earlier (Silvers 1973: 26–7), include the actor spitting out water on hearing 'shock' news; exercising a 'hammy' 'double take'; allowing their character to continue to chatter on before suddenly stopping to register surprising news etc. When these bits of 'business' are also poorly performed, the audience registers the falseness and lack of truth contained in the action above anything else. These are what Brett Mills refers to as the 'excess' that represents pejorative 'traditions of comic acting' (2010: 131, 137).

Equally, the audience response that is essential to comic meaning and to influencing effective comic acting can also become a danger to the comedian who works within the play format, if that performer over-emphasises the two-way performer/audience intercommunicative process at the expense of the dramatic interactions and to the detriment of Seyler's notion of 'balance'. Quite simply, expectation of a laugh can also become a pitfall for the comic performer, that is:

> When the remembered response of the audience becomes the principal sensation of doing the play, and one starts unconsciously to engineer the repetition of that response – stops, in fact, playing the truth, the character, the situation: starts in a word to ACT IN THE PAST, to recreate an effect. Then it stops being funny and one works harder and harder to bludgeon the audience into laughter.
>
> (Callow 1984: 169)

Interplay is contingent to the ephemeral circumstances of each and every live performance event, while maintaining a fragile state of truth is, ultimately another delicate balancing act for the comic actor to achieve. It is, however, a necessary tension for the actor to manage in balancing her/his performance within the exigencies that comic theatrical text requires. As the comic actor Richard Wilson star or *One Foot in The Grave* (BBC, 1990–2000) expresses it:

> I love comedy … because it is so satisfying. The laughter gives you a direct barometer of how you're doing with the audience, and that is a great sound. I don't have any special theory about comedy, other than it must be believable.
>
> (Wilson in Roose-Evans 1997: 213)

Creating interplay must feature within the comic actor's armoury of skills. It is an essential element in the manufacture and establishment of comic truth, itself a slippery and fragile state of theatricalised believability. The comic actor's mastery of audience interplay helps to realise the conditions for the intercommunicative state that allows for genuine laughter based on authentic recognition to ensue. Interplay is essential in creating complete comic meaning in live performance. Only then are the rules of the game fully established and its desired outcome enabled, when, as Halpern and Close note, 'where do the best laughs come from? Terrific connections made intellectually, or terrific revelations made emotionally' (2001: 25).

Whispering through the chink?

Perhaps the way in which interplay features in comic acting, might be illustrated in its most simple and basic form, by a description of how a comic actor used 'nothing' (or very little) to achieve audience laughter and enabled the laughter to continue, purely through interplay. In the following example, the phenomenon of the comic actor's use of a significant 'pause' is illustrated.

The dictionary definition of a pause is 'an interval of inaction … a break in speaking or action' (Pearsall and Trumble 1996: 1066). That is, 'dead air', which, in the context of a performance, might only become meaningful when the actor is intending to provoke an intended reaction from the audience. In drama, perhaps the most famous exponent of the pause was the playwright Harold Pinter. Use of the 'Pinteresque pause', has famously become widely redolent of 'subtextual', unspoken, 'deeper' meanings, often indicating some sense of 'menace', described elsewhere, as, for example, 'the impression of an unfinished feeling that can only be intuited but never known' (Krasner 2006: 525). Pinter himself referred to the 'silences' in his plays as:

> The thing known and unspoken … a language … where under what is said, another thing is being said … we communicate only too well, in our silence, in what is unsaid … a continual evasion, desperate rearguard attempts to keep ourselves to ourselves. Communication is too alarming.
>
> (Pinter 1981: 13–15)

The use of a pause as a peculiar means of signification might be said to illustrate – in microcosm – an aspect of Jacques Derrida's notion of '*différance*' – 'the gap between what a person speaks or writes and how that discourse is understood by its audience. The emphasis is on the gap and not the reception (Hussey 2010: 32).

Interestingly, perhaps, Derrida himself alluded to '*différance*' in the following, significant, terms, 'better, the play of difference, which, as Saussure reminded us, is the condition for the possibility and functioning of every sign, is in itself a silent play' (1982: 4).

In comic performance, a classic example of a comic actor's use of a pause within a live performance can be seen in the following example taken from the work of the American comedian Jack Benny (1894–1974). Benny was a hugely successful radio, television and film performer and the example is taken from his eponymous radio show, transmitted in 1948.

Benny himself wrote, nearly thirty years later, of 'a gag that got a terrific amount of nation-wide publicity and is still getting it whenever a columnist discusses the great jokes of the past' (Fein 1976: 44). By 1948, The Jack Benny Show (NBC/CBS, 1932–55) had been running on NBC for sixteen years using a quasi-domestic format that centred around Benny, his real-life wife, Mary Livingstone, his manservant Rochester (Eddie Anderson), various featured characters voiced by Mel Blanc and the contrived inclusion of famous celebrity guest artists. The comic moment that featured the pause 'gag' ran as follows:

Benny has been accosted by a robber
Robber: Don't make a move, this is a stickup. Now, come on. Your money or your life.
There is a pause. This leads to studio audience laughter that lasts for five seconds.
Robber: Look, bud! I said your money or your life!
Benny: I'm thinking it over!
Studio audience laughter for seven seconds.

(The Jack Benny Programme, NBC;
transcript from original broadcast of 28 March 1948)

Baldly stated, on paper, it is perhaps, difficult to see why this joke might evoke such a high level of audience laughter and achieve such notoriety, becoming, in Benny's own words, his 'most publicized laugh' (Benny et al. 1978: 171).

However, there are a number of features that made this gag so successful. First, there was Benny's familiarity to the audience. Benny was a well-established and reliable comic figure by this stage in his career. His comic persona and his perceived humorous foibles had become widely established and well-known to the public and his ongoing, personal popularity led to the show's increasingly high ratings. Benny's comic 'shtick' included a perception of stinginess with money and a kind of self-important pomposity – but despite (or, perhaps, partly because of) these perceived character flaws, his performed character retained an innate likeability. Benny's comic persona and characteristics were popular and achieved a high level of instant recognisability in the sense that 'actors who develop personae can become familiars, commonplaces, semiotic markers' (Sante and Holbrook Pierson 1999: xiii). The Benny character's legendary meanness, vanity and touchiness about his age had become emblematic signs of the individual performer and an associated core of his comic business. Consequently, the contemporary audience's reception of the pause only makes full sense if there is a foreknowledge of the Benny character's meanness. The silent interplay that features as part of Benny's execution of the pause and the audience's affective reaction to it also contains incongruity, in the sheer and absurd futility of Benny's apparent inner debate over his money or his life. The gag places the audience 'in the know' – they are aware of Benny's inner dilemma while the robber is not – and the audience is also placed in the position of the wiser and judgmental observer of the comic situation that unfolds. The actor/audience interplay is achieved through Benny's recognition of the audience's laughter response, his allowing the laughter to swell and ebb and, we must presume, through the quality of his facial reaction in response to the live studio audience during the entire twelve second dead air of the pauses. The factors that make this comic moment work so well relies on the acceptance of a kind of comic 'truth' that only really makes full and complete sense with this particular performer playing out this particular scenario in this particular way in front of this particular audience at that particular time.

While it is, of course, impossible to know exactly the nature of Benny's use of interplay or complicity with the live studio audience in this example, elsewhere, it is clear that Benny relied heavily on complicity to achieve his effects. Benny's friend and fellow comedian George Burns noted that Benny could get a laugh through 'doing' very little apart from indulging in a direct interplay with the audience, observing, 'Jack never does anything but stand there, touch his face, stare and then say "Well … " … the audience pushed Jack. The audience made "Well" a hit …' (in Benny et al. 1978: 93).

There is no doubt a large degree of expertise and timing evident in what Benny himself wrote of as this 'long pause – in fact one of my longest' (in Fein 1976: 144) but it is also clear that the audience's involvement – and Benny's attentiveness to that audience – are what made this moment where 'nothing' was happening, so satisfactory. It is a case of pure actor/audience interplay.

Conclusion: the comic actor as tightrope walker and juggler?

In conclusion, in a vital way, the phenomenon of 'doing and awareness' is acute for the comic actor who must stimulate, monitor and reflexively respond to the cues supplied by the audience's ongoing laughter. In that one important sense, in contrast to the introspective, internalising approach that characterises performance practice favoured in preponderant, modern, non-comic, 'method'-based forms of dramatic representation, comic performance requires a much more sophisticatedly reflexive, outward-looking and interpersonal approach. Comic acting is a particularly interactive category of performance in which the actors are overtly reliant on a two-way transmission of signification, as the laughter response mutually and reciprocally dictates the success, or otherwise, of the discourse. This more overtly interactive approach takes an organic and active form, in which the performers' ongoing measurement of the effectiveness of the performance – through the quantitative and qualitative monitoring of the response of audience laughter – is a hugely defining characteristic of the significance and success of the activity. In live comic performance, actors must be receptive to the occurrence, quality, nature and volume of laughter (and, of course, any lack thereof) and any other informative cues that they may receive from the audience. In recorded forms, in film, or in television or comedy where there may be no live audience, the imagined audience's response – including the leaving of pauses for expected laughter – must be taken into account. In this way, a non-present audience can still influence the overall discourse and the selected performance mode.

For the comic actor, moreover, Stanislavskian precepts of dramatic performative expression, in which there is a demand for performers to remain 'in character', leads to a situation where direct comic interplay with the audience becomes problematic for her/him to employ, particularly in performance modes in which breaking through the fourth wall is not an accepted part of the convention. In comedy, however, a 'contact' or connection is more explicitly entered into in a situation where the audience much more obviously and demonstrably 'assists' (Brook 1968: 156) and so, in establishing the intercommunicative practice through the direct response of their laughter, the audience is allowed a 'chink' in the fourth wall to be created, leading to a state where, the comic acting, hopefully, allows for the audience's input to shape the performance (becoming 'the wittiest partition, that ever I heard discourse, my Lord', in the words of Demetrius in *A Midsummer Night's Dream*, act 5, scene 1).

Comic acting relies on what Bernard Beckerman refers to as 'an acknowledged exchange between performer and spectator' (1990: 110) and as a differentiated system of dramatic communication, relies on interplay as the bridge to this acknowledged exchange. As is evident in the case of a stand-up comic: 'A live comedy show can best be described as consisting of a rich interaction between comedian and audience, in which the comedian's talk and the variety of audience responses are intricately woven' (McIlvenny et al. 1993: 239).

In walking the tightrope (while juggling) the audience interplay, finding chinks in the fourth wall and creating representations of truth within a heightened comic world, comic actors can surely be said to be the most skilled actors of all.

References

Aitken, M. (1996), *Style: Acting in High Comedy*, London: Applause.

Aston, E. and Savona, G. (1991), *Theatre as Sign-System: A Semiotics of Text and Performance*, London: Routledge.

Auslander, P. (2008), *Liveness: Performance in a Mediatized Culture*, Abingdon: Routledge.

Barker, R. (1988), *It's Hello from Him!* Sevenoaks: New English Library.

Bayliss, C. K., Maxfield, B. L., Millington, W. H., Gardner, F. and Watson Benedict, L. (2004), *The Project Gutenberg EBook of Philippine Folk-Tales*, chapter 7, accessed online at www.gutenberg.org/files/11028/11028-8.txt.

BBC (2005), Actor snaps over ringing mobile, 22 November, accessed online at http://news.bbc.co.uk/1/hi/england/london/4458810.stm.

Beckerman, B. (1990), *Theatrical Presentation: Performer, Audience and Act*, London: Routledge.

Benny, M. L., Marks, H. and Borie, M. (1978), *Jack Benny*, New York: Doubleday & Company.

Bergson, H. ([1900] 1994), Laughter. In W. Sypher, *Comedy*, Baltimore, MD: Johns Hopkins University Press.

Biner, P. (1972), *The Living Theatre,* New York: Avon.

Brockbank, P. (ed.) (1988), *Players of Shakespeare 1*, Cambridge: Cambridge University Press.

Brook, P. (1968), *The Empty Space*, Harmondsworth: Penguin.

Bryant, M. (2014), Violinist defended after she halted concert to tell off coughing child, *Evening Standard*, 4 December, p. 9.

Callow, S. (1984), *Being an Actor*, London: Methuen.

Callow, S. (1991), *Acting in Restoration Comedy*, New York: Applause Theatre Books.

Carr, J. and Greeves, L. (2007), *The Naked Jape*, London: Michael Joseph.

Cartledge, P. (1999), *Aristophanes and His Theatre of the Absurd*, London: Bristol Classical Press.

Cook, W. (1994), *Ha Bloody Ha: Comedians Talking*, London: Fourth Estate.

Coquelin, C. (1954), *The Art of the Actor*, London: George Allen & Unwin.

Corrigan, R. W. and Rosenberg, J. L. (eds.) (1964), *The Context and Craft of Drama*, San Francisco, CA: Chandler.

Cotes, P. (1989), *Sincerely Dickie: A Dickie Henderson Collection*, London: Robert Hale.

Derrida, J. (1982), Difference. In A. Bass (ed.) (1082), *Margins of Philosophy*, Chicago, IL: University of Chicago Press, accessed online at www.stanford.edu/class/history34q/readings/Derrida/Differance.html.

Diderot, D. (1758) *De la poésie dramatique*, chapter XI, accessed online at http://lettres.spip.ac-rouen.fr/IMG/pdf/mise_en_scene.pdf.

Double, O. (1997), *Stand-up: On Being A Comedian*, London: Methuen.

Durrenmatt, F. (1964), Problems of the Theatre. In R. W. Corrigan and J. L. Rosenberg (eds.), *The Context and Craft of Drama*, San Francisco, CA: Chandler.

Emigh J. and Emigh, U. (1986), Hajari Bhand of Rajasthan: a joker in the deck, *The Drama Review* 30(1): 101–30, accessed online at www.jstor.org/discover/10.2307/1145716?uid=3738032&uid=2&uid=4&sid=21104650029961.

Fein, I. A. (1976), *Jack Benny: An Intimate Biography*, London: W. H. Allen.

Fisher, J. (1975), *George Formby*, London: Woburn-Futura.

Freud, S. ([1905] 1964), *Jokes and Their Relation to the Unconscious*, London: Hogarth Press.

Fry, S. (2010), *The Fry Chronicles: An Autobiography*, London: Michael Joseph.

Giannachi, G. and Luckhurst, M. (1999), *On Directing: Interviews with Directors*, London: Faber & Faber.

Gielgud, J. (1965), *Stage Directions*, London: Mercury.

Glasgow, R. D. V. (1995), *Madness, Masks, and Laughter: An Essay on Comedy*, London: Associated University Presses.

Goodwin, C. (1986), Audience diversity, participation and interpretation, *Text* 6(3): 283–316.

Graves, G. (1931), *Gaieties and Gravities: The Autobiography of a Comedian*, London: Hutchison and Co.

Greig, J. Y. T. (1969), *The Psychology of Laughter and Comedy*, New York: Cooper Square.

Gruber, W. (1986), *Comic Theaters*, Athens, GA: University of Georgia.

Halliwell, L. (1987), *Double Take and Fade Away*, London: Grafton Books.

Halpern, C. and Close, D. (2001), *Truth in Comedy*, Colorado Springs, CO: Meriwether.

Hawthorne, N. (2002), *Straight Face*, London: Sceptre.

Hethmon, R. (1966), *Strasberg at the Actors Studio*, London: Jonathan Cape.

Hussey, A. (2010), Stories of a serious man [review of D. Mikics, *Who Was Jacques Derrida? An Intellectual Biography*], *The Independent*, 9 April 2010.

Jarvis, Martin (2003), *Broadway Jeeves? The Diary of a Theatrical Adventure*, London: Methuen.

Kirby, M. (1987), *A Formalist Theatre*, Philadelphia, PA: University of Pennsylvania Press.

Krasner, D. (2006), Harold Pinter and the twilight of modernism, *Theatre Journal* 58(3): 524–6.

Lahr, J. (2001), *Show and Tell: New Yorker Profiles*, London: Bloomsbury.

McIlvenny, P., Mettovaara, S. and Tapio, R. (1993), I Really Wanna Make You Laugh: Stand-Up Comedy and Audience Response. In M. Suojanen and K. Kulkki-Nieminen (eds), *Folia, Femistica and Linguistica: Proceedings of the Annual Finnish Linguistics Symposium*, Tampere: Finnish and General Linguistics Dept, Tampere University.

Medhurst, A. (2003), *A National Joke: Popular Comedy and English Identities*, London: Routledge.

Mellencamp, P. (1986), Situation Comedy, Feminism and Freud: Discourses of Gracie and Lucy. In T. Modleski (ed.), *Studies in Entertainment: Critical Approaches to Mass Culture*, Bloomington, IN: Indiana University Press.

Miles-Brown, J. (2000), *Acting: A Drama Studio Source Book*, London: Peter Owen.

Mills, B. (2005), *Television Sitcom*, London: BFI Publishing

Mills, B. (2010), Contemporary comedy performance in British sitcom. In C. Cornea (ed.), *Genre and Performance: Film and Television*, Manchester: Manchester University Press.

Monkhouse, B. (1998), *Over the Limit: My Secret Diaries 1993–8*, London: Century.

Moore, S. (1974), *The Stanislavski System: the Professional Training of an Actor*, New York: Viking Press.

Morreall, J. (ed.) (1987), *The Philosophy of Laughter and Humor*, New York: Albany.

O'Brien, M. E. (1983), *Film Acting: The Techniques and History Of Acting For The Camera*, New York: Acro Publishing.

Parsons, N. (1994), *The Straight Man: My Life in Comedy*, London: Weidenfeld and Nicolson.

Pearsall, J. and Trumble, B. (1996), *The Oxford English Reference Dictionary*, Oxford: Oxford University Press.

Pinter, H. (1981), Writing for the theatre. In H. Pinter, *Plays: One*, London: Methuen.

Provine, R. R. (2000), *Laughter: A Scientific Investigation*, London: Faber & Faber.

Purdie, S. (1993), *Comedy: The Mastery of Discourse*, Hemel Hempstead: Harvester Wheatsheaf.

Raskin, V. (1985), *Semiotic Mechanisms of Humor*, Dordrecht: D. Reidel Publishing Company.

Redgrave, M. (1995), *The Actor's Ways and Means*, London: Nick Hern Books.

Ritchie, C. (2006), *The Idler and the Dandy in Stage Comedy*, London: Edwin Mellen.

Roose-Evans, J. (1997), *One Foot On The Stage: The Biography of Richard Wilson*, London: Orion.

Russell Brown, J. (1993), *Shakespeare's Plays in Performance*, New York: Applause Theatre Books.

Rutherford, M. (1972), *Margaret Rutherford: An Autobiography*, London: W. H. Allen.

Sante, L. and Holbrook Pierson, M. (1999), *OK You Mugs: Writers on Movie Actors*, New York: Pantheon Books.

Schopenhauer, A. (1907), *The World as Will and Idea*, 6th edition, trans. R. B. Haldane and J. Kemp, London: Routledge & Kegan Paul.

Seyler, A. (1990), *The Craft of Comedy*, London: Nick Hern Books.

Silvers, P. (1973), *This Laugh is On Me*, New Jersey: Prentice Hall.

Stanislavski, C. ([1936] 1986), *An Actor Prepares*, London: Methuen.

Thomson, P. (2000), *On Actors and Acting*, Exeter: University of Exeter.

Walker, T. (2011), And now, back to the studio …, *The Independent*, 2 February.

Wright, J. (2007), *Why Is That So Funny?* New York: Limelight.

2

STRAIGHT LINE/WAVY LINE

Steve Kaplan

We've been told that comedy is about a straight man and a comic. A funny guy who says and does funny things, and a straight man—someone who can act as a foil to the comic, and occasionally sing a song.

But comedy isn't dependent on a straight man and a comic. That's not to say there haven't been many great comedy duos: Laurel and Hardy; Burns and Allen; Abbott and Costello; Hope and Crosby; Tracy and Hepburn; Lewis and Martin. However, the dynamic at work in these teams is not simply that of the straight man shoveling set-ups to the funny clown. The reality is that comedy is teamwork, and each member of that team plays a vital part in the comic scenario.

Rather than straight man and comic, the term that I use is *straight line/wavy line*. The dynamic of straight line/wavy line is the idea that comedy isn't us watching somebody do something funny, but rather us watching someone watch someone do something funny. We use the term straight line because the character in the scene is behaving as though they're traveling in a straight line with blinders on, not noticing what's going on around them. The straight line is usually blind to the problem, or creating, contributing, or exacerbating it. The term wavy line describes the character's struggle in scene. On the one hand, they're aware of the problem, but on the other hand, they're confused as to what to do about it. On the one hand and on the other hand. And back and forth and back and forth, struggling with the problem but unable to solve it (because he or she is a non-hero, someone who lacks some, if not all, essential skills required to solve the problem).

One sees, one doesn't

The first element of Straight/Wavy is that one character "sees," and the other is blind. The best way to demonstrate this would be to take a look at a sketch by what we would consider to be the quintessential straight man and comic. That would be, arguably, Abbott and Costello. Costello was the comic in the duo, and Abbott was the quintessential straight man, and without a doubt their most famous routine was their classic bit, "Who's on First?" (Because of comedy's essential performative nature, it's best if you watch the routine on video as well as follow along in the text. Abbott and Costello performed this routine hundreds of times, and there are multiple versions available on the internet.[1]

Abbott and Costello are at the baseball field.

Abbott: Strange as it may seem, they give ballplayers nowadays very peculiar names.

Costello: Funny names?

Abbott: Nicknames. Now on the St. Louis team we have Who's on first, What's on second, I Don't Know's on third—

Costello: That's what I want to find out. I want you to tell me the names of the fellas on the St. Louis team.

Abbott: I'm telling you, Who's on first, What's on second, I Don't Know's on third.

Costello: You know the fellas' names?

Abbott: Yes.

Costello: Well, then who's playing first?

Abbott: Yes.

Costello: I mean the fella's name on first base.

Abbott: Who.

Costello: The fella playing first base for St. Louis.

Abbott: Who.

Costello: The guy on first base.

Abbott: Who is on first!

Costello: Well, what are you askin' me for?

Abbott: I'm not asking you, I am telling you. Who is on first.

Costello: I'm asking YOU—who's on first?

Abbott: That's the man's name.

Costello: That's who's name?

Abbott: Yes.

Costello: Well go ahead and tell me.

Abbott: Who.

Costello: The guy on first.

Abbott: Who!

Costello: The first baseman.

Abbott: Who is on first.

Costello: Have you got a first baseman on first?
Abbott: Certainly.
Costello: Then who is playing first?
Abbott: Absolutely.
Costello: When you pay the off first baseman every month, who gets the money?
Abbott: Every dollar of it. And why not, the man's entitled to it.
Costello: Who is?
Abbott: Yeah.
Costello: So who gets it?
Abbott: Why shouldn't he? Sometimes his wife comes down and collects it.
Costello: Whose wife?
Abbott: Yes.
Pause while Costello makes some frustrated noises.

One of these guys is blind and one sees. At first blush, you might think that Abbott "sees" and Costello is "blind": Abbott has all the information and Costello doesn't know the names of the players and can't keep up with Abbott. But a closer look reveals that Abbott is the one who doesn't see. What he doesn't see is that he's confusing Costello. With a more perceptive Abbott, perhaps the conversation goes this way:

Costello: You know the fellows' names?
Abbott: Yes.
Costello: Well, then who's playing first?
Abbott: Yes.
Costello: I mean the fellow's name on first base.
Abbott: Wait. I can see what's confusing you. It's because the names are strange, like Sam Who and Joe What. I know it's crazy. Get it? It sounds like I'm asking you "who?" but I'm just telling you his last name.
Costello: Oh. Thanks.

Not so funny, right? The comedy depends upon Abbott's *inability to see* exactly what's confusing Costello. If Abbott saw the source of the confusion, he'd have to correct him, right? So the only way that the routine could work is for Abbott not to notice. He's blind to what's confusing Costello.

Even if Abbott is "blind," how can we say that Costello is the one who "sees"? After all, Costello is an idiot, a fool in the classic sense. How do I know that Costello sees? Because Costello is about to learn about third base.

Costello: All I'm trying to find out is what's the guy's name on first base?!
Abbott: No, what is on second!
Costello: I'm not asking you who's on second!
Abbott: Who is on first.
Costello: That's what I am trying to find out.

Abbott: Then don't change the players around.

Costello: I'm not changing nobody. What's the guy's name on first base?

Abbott: What's the guy's name on second base.

Costello: I'm NOT asking you who's on second!

Abbott: Who's on first.

Costello: I don't know.

Abbott: Oh, he's on third. We're not talking about him.

Costello rolls his eyes in frustration and hits the bat in his hand.

Costello: How did I get on third base?

Abbott: Well, you mentioned his name.

Costello: If I mentioned the third baseman's name, who did I say's playing third?

Abbott: No, Who is playing first.

Costello: Stay off of first, would ya?

Abbott: Well, what do you want me to do?

Costello: What's the guy's name on third base?

Abbott: What's on second.

Costello: I'm *not* asking you who's on second.

Abbott: Who is on first.

Costello: I don't know.

Abbott: He's on third.

Costello: There I go back on third again.

Abbott: Well I can't change their names.

Costello: Would ya please stay on third base, Mister Broadhurst.

Abbott: Now what is it you want to know?

Costello: What is the fella's name on third base?

Abbott: What is the fella's name on second base.

Costello: I'm *not asking you who's on second*!

Abbott: Who's on first.

Costello: I don't know.

Both: (*quickly*) Third base!

Costello makes another weird noise in exasperation, like steam out of a kettle

So Costello's beginning to pick up on it. He doesn't know why, but every time he says "I don't know" Abbott comes right back with "Third base." He just doesn't know how to make sense of it. Maybe if he were smarter, he could put it all together. But he's not—he's a non-hero.[2] Yet he sees it. He's aware of things. If you watch the clip, you'll also notice that as Costello gets more and more frustrated, he also becomes more and more animated: emitting odd noises, flailing about, at one point seemingly screwing himself into the ground while steam practically vents from the top of his head. If comedy tells the truth, why are all these vaudeville turns so funny (and to me, they are.) It's because the wavy line has the obligation to express his internal reality. All those comic noises are the external expression of an internal truth. If you could put a sound and a movement to frustration, that's what it would look like.

Costello: You got an outfield?
Abbott: Oh sure.
Costello: St. Louis has got a good outfield?
Abbott: Oh, absolutely.
Costello: The left fielders name?
Abbott: Why.
Costello: *(bouncing up and down)* I don't know, I just thought I'd ask ya.
Abbott: Well I just thought I'd tell ya.
Costello: Then tell me who is playing left field.
Abbott: *Who* is playing first.
Costello: Stay out of the infield!
Abbott: Don't mention the names out here.
Costello: I want to know what's the fella's name in left field.
Abbott: What is on second.
Costello: I'm not asking you who's on second.
Abbott: *Who* is on first.
Costello: I don't know.
Both: Third base.
Costello winds up and makes more noises in his deep frustration.

Of the two, Abbott and Costello, who do you find yourself caring about? Who has your emotional attention? For almost all of us, it's poor, struggling Costello. That's what the wavy line does. The wavy line has our emotional focus, because the wavy line is our representative on stage or screen. He's us in the scenario. He is the human being in the story.

The French philosopher Henri Bergson, in his essay "Laughter," posited that comedy is "something mechanical encrusted on the living." "By mechanical" Bergson means the stubborn, plodding, inflexible, customary, as well as the traditional—those things in human experience that repeat unthinkingly, systematically, forming a counterbalance to the natural vibrancy of human life" (Belz 2007: 7–8). In other words, someone acting mechanically, like a machine, creates comedy. But Bergson is only half right, because as John Cleese and the rest of the Pythons discovered, comedy was someone watching someone doing something silly (or mechanically), as opposed to simply the silly person and his/her mechanical actions. There always needs to be a human being in the scenario, reacting to or struggling against the mechanical.

Abbott: Take it easy, take it easy man.
Costello: And the left fielder's name?
Abbott: Why.
Costello: Because.
Abbott: Oh he's center field.
Costello hits himself on the head again and knocks the hat off for a second time.
Abbott: Would you pick up your hat? Please. Pick up your hat.

Costello runs and picks up his hat.
Costello: I want to know what's the pitcher's name.
Abbott: What's on second!
Costello: I don't know.
The both point at each other as they say ...
Both: Third base!

Costello learns that, for some unexplained reason, every time he says, "I don't know," Abbott will say, "third base." He learns so well, in fact, that he can begin anticipating "third base" as soon as the phrase "I don't know" is uttered. Costello "sees" the information that Abbott is giving him and struggles with the logical paradoxes. The wavy line's subtext might go like this: "On the one hand, I'm getting answers to my questions, on the other hand, the answers make no sense, on the other hand, I'm learning the answers to the players' names, on the other hand, who can make head or tails of this? I don't know, he's on third!"

Costello: You gotta catcher?
Abbott: Yes.
Costello: Catcher's name?
Abbott: Today.
Costello: Today. And tomorrow's pitching?
Abbott: Now you've got it.
Costello: That's all, St. Louis has got a couple of days on the team, that's all.
Abbott: Well I can't help that.
Costello gets even more frustrated and starts shaking and making noises.
Abbott: Alright. What do you want me to do?
Costello is almost to tears.
Costello: Got a catcher?
Abbott: Yes.
Costello: I'm a good catcher too, ya know?
Abbott: I know that.
Costello: I would like to play for the St. Louis team.
Abbott: Well I'm not going to arrange that, I ...
Costello: I would like to catch! Now, I'm being a good catcher, Tomorrow is pitching on the team and I'm catching.
Abbott: Yes.
Costello: Tomorrow throws the ball and the guy up bunts the ball, now when he bunts the ball, me being a good catcher, I wanna throw the guy out at first base, so I pick up the ball and throw it to who?
Abbott: Now that's the first thing you've said right.
Costello: I don't even know what I'm talking about!

The wavy line is the one who sees, and that in and of itself can create comedy. David Wieck in his essay "Funny Things" states that in a joke structure, if we "set aside questions of psychology, or content, and questions about why we laugh … what is left is the fact that there is a defect or wrongness in the form of what we perceive" (Wieck 1967: 442). The wavy line sees that defect, and the observer's resulting confusion and/or bewilderment creates the comic moment. As William Goldman points out in his book *Which Lie Did I Tell*, "The core of the comedy is based on embarrassment. A great deal of the laughter comes from the figure who is really doing nothing. Billy Crystal just sits there, first confused, then intrigued, then stunned at Meg Ryan's behavior. Ben Stiller gets huge laughs just standing, huddled, facing the corner of the bathroom as nightmares swirl all around him" (Goldman 2000: 161).

Abbott and Costello and Jerry and George

With Abbott and Costello, the comic Costello is the wavy line, and the straight man Abbott is the straight line. So would that relationship be the same in a contemporary comedy, say *Seinfeld*? In *Seinfeld*, who would be the "funny" ones and who would be the straight man? We would usually consider the straight man to be Jerry, with Kramer and George as the funny ones. The following is a scene from "The Abstinence," from the eighth season of *Seinfeld*.[3]

Jerry's apartment. George is sitting on the couch watching Jeopardy and playing with a Rubik's cube while Jerry is talking to him from the kitchen area.
Jerry: Fire drill, can you believe that?
George: Who is Pericles?
Alex Trebek: (O.S.) Pericles is correct.
Jerry: Like fire in a school is such a big deal.
Kramer enters the apartment.
Kramer: You got any matches?
Jerry: Middle drawer.
George: Who is Sir Arthur Conan Doyle?
Alex Trebek: (O.S.) We were looking for "Who is Sir Arthur Conan Doyle."

We can see that George is blind to the fact that, all of a sudden, he's smart!

Kramer: Thanks.
Kramer leaves.
The phone rings. Jerry picks it up.
Jerry: Hello.
Katie: (O.S.) Jerry.
Jerry: Oh hi, Katie.
Kramer enters again.
Kramer: Ashtray?
Jerry: No, I don't have any ashtrays.
Kramer: Ooh, cereal bowls.

Katie: Jerry, now don't freak out, I'll take care of it.
Jerry: No, Katie, don't—
Jerry hangs up the phone.
Kramer: All right, thanks.
Kramer runs out.
George: What is Tungsten or Wolfram?
Alex Trebek: We were looking for "What is Tungsten, or Wolfram."
Jerry: Is this a repeat?

Jerry, who up until this point has been distracted with Kramer running in and out and trying to get his neurotic agent off the phone realizes that George, George mind you, has been getting the answers right. Not just some of the answers. Not just most. *All the answers.* When you watch the scene, what you notice is that Jerry is constantly pivoting his attention between Kramer, who's creating a smoker's haven in his apartment, Katie, his crazy agent, and George. Jerry sees it all, and can't help but be distracted and just a little bit confused by it all. Kramer, George and Katie all seem to be on their own tracks though. Even though Jerry is the straight man, in this part of the scene, he's the wavy line. The wavy line sees what's in its environment but struggles with it, can't solve it because the wavy line is a non-hero. The straight line doesn't see any problem, because more often than not, the straight line is creating the problem. George is straight. He doesn't see that he's now a genius. Jerry sees everything, back and forth between his agent on the phone, Kramer wanting ashtrays but taking cereal bowls, George nailing the questions from *Jeopardy*. The wavy line goes back and forth, with multiple points of focus.

George gets up and walks into the kitchen.
George: No, no, no. Just lately, I've been thinking a lot clearer. Like this afternoon, *(to television)* What is chicken Kiev, *(to Jerry)* I really enjoyed watching a documentary with Louise.

George has, up to this point, been oblivious to all the comings and goings in the apartment, oblivious to Kramer and his odd need for ashtrays, even oblivious to the fact that he's now become a genius. He's the straight line. Jerry, struggling with the phone call, the intrusive and insistent neighbor and his dunce of a best friend who now amazingly knows all the answers, is the wavy line. Kramer and George are doing something silly. Jerry is watching them do something silly. We're watching Jerry watch them do something silly.

Jerry: Louise! That's what's doin' it. You're no longer pre-occupied with sex, so your mind is able to focus.

The wavy line struggles, but when the struggle ends, so does the comic beat. The dynamic of straight line/wavy line is *a function of focus, not character*; there is no such thing as a "wavy" character or a "straight" character. It's a matter of focus. The wavy line struggles, and as it struggles, even slightly, it captures our attention and our sympathies. Beat by beat, moment by moment, second by second, the focus can, and does, change, and as it changes, so does our focus, our attention and our emotional attachment to the characters.

Right now we're about to see the focus switch from Jerry to George.

George: *(looking up)* You think?

That's the first time in the scene that George turns his head to really look at Jerry, as George literally looks up and pays attention in the scene. George now takes focus and becomes the wavy line. And throughout the next few lines, George is constantly maintaining two points of focus: toward Jerry, then looking away, then again towards Jerry, and then looking away. This multiple focus, this second cousin to the double take, is the wavy line, as George is literally struggling with the new concept of his no-sex genius. Meanwhile, Jerry, having solved his problem, is now the straight line. He's not reacting to George's confusion, or embarrassment, or humiliation. Jerry is quite amusing, but it's George, for the moment, that has our emotional attention.

Jerry: Yeah. I mean, let's say this is your brain.
Jerry holds a lettuce head.
Jerry: Okay, from what I know about you, your brain consists of two parts: the intellect, represented here …
Jerry pulls off tiny piece of lettuce.
Jerry: … and the part obsessed with sex.
Jerry shows large piece.
Jerry: Now granted, you have extracted an astonishing amount from this little scrap.
George reacts with a kind of a "hey it was nothing" little grin and shrug.
Jerry: But with no-sex-Louise, this previously useless lump, is now functioning for the first time in its existence.
Jerry eats tiny piece of lettuce.
George: Oh my God. I just remembered where I left my retainer in second grade. I'll see ya.
George throws the finished Rubik's cube to a bewildered Jerry and he exits.

George again goes back to being kind of an idiot, and Jerry's confusion makes him, again, a wavy line. So it goes, back and forth and back and forth.

Focus, not character

The focus can, and must, shift from character to character as they take center stage in the emotional story—not necessarily the character with the biggest part or the funniest jokes or the part with the most screen time, stage time or dialogue, but the character who, at that moment, has our emotional focus. It's important to remember that there is no such thing as a straight line character or a wavy line character. Straight line/wavy line is focusing device, not a characterization technique, and as such, is applied or observed on a beat-by-beat basis. As we follow the characters around, especially in sitcoms, characters come in and out of focus. In *Everybody Loves Raymond*, for example, if Frank does something stupid, you'll watch Ray seeing him do it. A moment later, Ray does something stupid, with Debra shooting him a withering look. In the next scene, Ray desperately tries to talk his way out of a tight spot (wavy line) while Debra just stares at him (straight line). You'll notice that she doesn't react to *every* one of Ray's fevered attempts to get something by her. In the next beat, Ray says something stupid and thinking it's done the trick, exits (straight line), while Debra just looks at him, shaking her head, too confounded to speak (wavy line).

Part of the reason for this focusing dynamic is because, unlike other art forms, comedy is the only one that requires a specific physiological reaction (i.e. laughter) from a large number of strangers—not once or twice, but eighty, ninety, one hundred times over the course of a couple of hours or it's thought to be a failure. Not other art form requires that kind of uniform response. Drama? You wouldn't expect to see a thousand people sitting watching *A Streetcar Named Desire* to all reach into their pocket and pull out a hankie and cry simultaneously at the end of the play. That would be weird. It would be comic, in fact. You wouldn't expect a hundred people walking into the Louvre to see La Pieta to all say "Ah!" and have the same astonished look of awe all at the same time. Yet, if a hundred, or five hundred, or a thousand people don't share the same physiological response sixty or seventy or eighty times in an evening, then that comedy is said to be a failure. And that requires an immense amount of focus.

It's also why a comedy might be funny on a Thursday, but die a quiet death on Sunday. When I was producing live theater, it used to drive me crazy. Why were their reactions so different night to night? And actors would come off stage and say, boy, what a terrible audience that was. And yet, I was in that audience. And I didn't think I was terrible. I thought I was as prepared to laugh as always. I might not laugh as loud since I knew the jokes, but I was prepared to enjoy it. And I started to see something different. Something happened on those nights when it didn't work. It wasn't just the audience. Something was happening.

Let's say there's a play in which two actors are down there doing a joke, and there are three spear carriers up here. And one night, just as they do the joke and get a big laugh, this spear carrier scratches his nose and hears a big laugh. What does that actor now think? Boy! I really got a big laugh out of my nose scratch.

So what might that spear carrier do the next night? Make it bigger! Because he wasn't even trying before. The following night he really gives the nose a good old scratch. Which distracts a portion of the audience, so the laugh is smaller than the previous night. So now the laugh is half as big as on the first night. So the next night, the spear carrier makes the nose scratch even bigger (louder, faster, funnier). By the end of the weekend, the laugh is totally gone.

OK, maybe it didn't happen as overtly as that. But I did start to see differences between performances that worked and performances that fell flat. The story was the same, the jokes were the same, so what was different? Maybe on those flat nights, the characters seemed to have too many skills (*non-hero*: lacking in some, if not all the required skills with which to win), or played negative actions (*positive action*: the idea that with *every* action, your character actually thinks it might just work), or faked emotions (*active emotion*: the idea that the best emotional beats to play are the emotions that are actually occurring naturally to the actor right there, *at that moment*, on stage or set). Or they might have forgotten what the comic point of the scene was and unconsciously stole focus. There's an apocryphal story about an actor who was playing the Doctor in the first production of *A Streetcar Named Desire*. The Doctor is the character who comes on in the end to take poor Blanche away. He meets a friend on the street, and the friend stops to congratulate him being in a big hit Broadway show. "What's the play about?" the friend asks. Practically bursting with pride, the actor replies, "Well, it's about this doctor who comes to help this poor lady to …"

Now this story probably never happened, but the point is that whatever the actor who actually played the Doctor thought, it wouldn't have hurt the drama. A thousand people could be sitting in a theatre watching *A Streetcar Named Desire* and one could be watching Stella, another could be watching Blanche, still another could be focused on Stanley, and you could be paying attention to the Doctor (maybe you're his mother.) The point is that they could all be watching somebody different in the scenario, and each still get a valid emotional experience from the end of the play. But … if you're watching a comedy and you're supposed to watching Felix and Oscar, but somehow your attention is distracted and you're paying attention to the spear carrier, you could miss the joke. Because the spear carrier doesn't understand the function of comedy. Comedy's about teamwork. It's not about one person being funny.

Unless everyone on the team is all dedicated to creating the same comic moment, and helps the audience focus on that moment, the comic moment will be diminished or lost. Straight line/wavy line dynamic helps to create that focus.

Even in film or TV, where the camera tells you where to look, the camera still has to show you the most important thing, which is not the funny line, but a character's reaction to that line. Not someone saying something funny, but some human being's reaction to seeing something silly.

The sad part, though, is that many people still believe that's the way comedy is structured. I had a friend who used to be on this sitcom, which shall remain unnamed, headlined by a stand-up comic, who also shall remain unnamed. My friend told me that they would come in on a Monday, for the table read. Everyone would be there: stars, co-stars, writers, network people. And there would be a fair sprinkling of comedy lines, punch lines, all throughout the script to a variety of characters. And then this not-to-be-named Star would storm upstairs and then demand the writers to follow her. This happened every week. And the Star would—somehow—figure out a way whereby on Wednesday, all the lines that people laughed at in the table read were now the star's lines. Because it was the star's impression—and this is a talented, experienced stand-up comic—that comedy is about the person who says the funny line.

And there are still people out there, week in, week out, who grab punch lines from co-stars and day players so that they have all the funny things to say. Because people still think that the funny person is the one with all the funny lines.

The wavy line is us

The wavy line is our representative on stage, which has many ramifications. To illustrate, let me share a scene from the great, late HBO sketch show *Mr. Show*, starring Bob Odenkirk and David Cross. In this sketch, "The Burgundy Loaf," David Cross plays a man on a date with his girlfriend at a very fancy restaurant, and Bob Odenkirk plays the overbearing French Maître D'.[4]

In an upscale restaurant, The Burgundy Loaf, a man and a woman are having a romantic dinner.

Woman:	This is so sweet.
Man:	Yeah, this is classy huh?
Woman:	This restaurant is fantastic.
Man:	Yeah, they gave it another star. Six stars, it means "the ultimate dining experience." For "the ultimate lady experience."

The Maître D' carrying a white towel over his arm comes up to the table.

Maître D':	I trust everything is to Monsieur's satisfaction?
Man:	Oh, yeah, it's incredible, it's great.

Note that in the beginning there is *no straight line/wavy line*. You don't always have to have a straight/wavy dynamic. In this case, the beginning is just the exposition, setting up the given circumstances in the scene. You might not have straight/wavy because it's a shared scene, or a serious scene, or no one person is struggling with a problem in the scene. Straight line/wavy line, like all the tools, are just that—simply tools you can use to heighten the comic elements in a narrative.

Woman:	Sweety, will you excuse me, for just a moment? I'm just going to wash my hands.
Maître D':	Nonsense, Madame. *(claps his hands)* Le "hand-washier"!

A man wearing a white jacket comes out from the kitchen with a crystal bowl and a towel.
He bends at the knee so she can wash her hands without leaving the table.
Woman: Wow, how fancy!
Maître D':   Do Madame and Monsieur require anything else?
Man: No, we're good.

What are the "givens" here? A couple are having dinner at a fancy restaurant. How fancy? The fanciest. So fancy the restaurant's got six stars, one more star than is even possible. Plus, the restaurant has an unusual feature—it provides the ultimate in service of every kind, without the customers ever having to leave their seats. And like all good sketches, the writers take this premise to its ultimate logical, yet absurd, conclusion.

Maître D':   Very well, I shall bring your entrees. *(claps his hands)* Entrees duet!
Two other servers come out from the kitchen and place the entrees on the table.
Man: Oh boy, alright.
Woman: Ooh! Wow!
The man wipes his mouth and begins to stand up.
Maître D':   Sir, is there a problem?
Man: No, just where are the restrooms?
Maître D':   Ah. No.
Man: No, uh, I mean, the men's room.
Maître D':   Shh, shh, sir, please. We do not have such a thing. The Burgundy
             Loaf prides itself as the epitome of class and distinction. And we
             would not soil our atmosphere with a men's toilet room. It's too
             crudité to imagine.
Woman: Couldn't you just hold it in?
Man: No, I can't!
Maître D':   Ah, Madame, Monsieur, everything is taken care of.
The Maître D' comes around and pats the man's chair for him to sit.
As the man is about the sit, the Maître D' pulls off the cushion to reveal a toilet bowl ready
for use.
Maître D':   Voila! Le "chair." Crafted from Brazilian mahogany.
The Maître D' claps again.
Maître D':   "Le box"!
The man with the white coat comes out of the back room with a wooden box and hands it
to the Maître D'.
The Maître D' shows the man and the woman.
Maître D':   Le "box," hand-crafted with Italian gold leaf. *(opens the box)* Inside, a
             velvet lining to cradle monsieur's leavings with the tender delicacy
             of a devoted mother.
The Maître D' clears his throat and places the box under the toilet seat.
Maître D':   Monsieur may sit, enjoy his meal and perform his task at leisure.
Man: You want me to shit in a box while I'm eating dinner?

It should be obvious that the wavy line is David Cross. What I want you to note is *how little you have to do to play the wavy line.* You don't have to have clever dialogue, or unrealistic behavior. Because the wavy line is just reacting as our representative, as us, and when the wavy line does speak, his dialogue, and performance, just has to be simple, direct and honest. "You want me to shit in a box while I'm eating dinner?" It ain't Moliere. Or Milton Berle or Jerry Lewis. And it doesn't have to be. You don't need to strain for "comic behavior" for the wavy line. How you behave is what you might actually do in that given situation.

Before you say, "Well, I would *never* do that, Mr. Kaplan!" let's rewind and take a look at this beat again.

Maître D':   Monsieur may sit, enjoy his meal and perform his task at leisure.

Now before he says anything, he looks at the girlfriend. He looks at the box. He looks at the maître D'. He'll look at the couple behind him. He's struggling inside the gap between expectation and reality. And note that the girlfriend doesn't see anything wrong with the box. She's a straight line. She's blind to creating the problem. Straight lines often achieve their expectations, meaning that since her expectation is that this is a wonderful restaurant, she doesn't see anything wrong with having her date shit in a box during dinner.

Man: You want me to shit in a box while I'm eating dinner?

Why doesn't he leave? This is disgusting—you've got to shit in a box? Why doesn't he just leave? Because if he left, it would mean he had skills that would make him a hero, someone who is strong-willed enough not to be intimidated by a sniffy French maître D'. But our guy, our non-hero is trying to impress his girl. And, hey, the restaurant has six stars. When's the last time he ate at a six-star restaurant? For all he knows, shitting in a box while you're eating is what *everyone* is doing nowadays! So why not?

What would happen to the comedy if the girl said, no, I don't want to do that, you don't have to do that? The focus would be defused and the problem would no longer be an absurd, ridiculous situation, it would just be some unlikeable situation that you can choose to do or not to do. The fact is that everybody in the scenario is a straight line except for David Cross. He looks over at the girlfriend, and does she any problem with this? No. So that traps him even more.

Maître D':   When Monsieur is "en vacant," we will deliver the box to his home
              first class, courtesy of the Burgundy Loaf.
The Maître D' starts to undo the man's pants. The man stops him and the Maître D' stands back, proper. He gestures for the man to take his seat.
The man looks at his date in confusion, then to the Maître D' smiling nervously.
The Maître D' makes some noises—French-like—while gesturing for the man to sit again.

The man looks around the dining room.
The Maître D' clears his throat and gestures again for the man to sit.
The man starts to undo his pants very slowly. Finally he does.
The Maître D' gestures again.
The man drops his pants completely. The Maître D' gestures one last time.
The man is now sitting on the toilet seat with his pants down, ready to go.

The way to develop any premise, from sketch to feature is to take the problem and make bigger. With a wavy line, a good technique is simply to add more points of focus.

The Maître D' takes out a whistle and blows it.
Maître D': Rudy!
Rudy, a man in a white jacket and tie enters from the kitchen.
Maître D': Rudy will await your foundation. Enjoy your meal.
Rudy takes out a flashlight and bends to one knee behind the man, next to the box.
The man looks at him in shock, then to the Maître D' and finally his date.
The woman is enjoying her meal.
Woman: The sea bass is excellent.
The man looks back at Rudy who is looking under the seat for the man's poop, then back at her.

When I watch this clip with audiences, there's a lot of laughter at this point. No dialogue, just laughter. No jokes, just David Cross, looking at the girl, about to speak, then looking back at Rudy looking up his butt with a flashlight, then to the Maître D', then back to Rudy. You don't need to worry about jokes or acting "funny." The comedy comes from the wavy line struggling to solve an unsolvable problem. Simply by creating the straight/wavy dynamic relieves you of the obligation to write witticisms, or invent comic behavior. Just put a character like us (or maybe a little less than us) trying to deal with a situation that's impossible to deal with. At the same time, the straight line character is blind to the absurdity or his own ridiculous behavior. We say that the straight line achieves his expectations—that is, the girlfriend expects this to be a wonderful, romantic evening, and nothing that she sees, including her date having to shit where he eats, conflicts with that.

Woman: This cream sauce is so light. I can't wait to meet your parents.
Man: Uh, yeah.
Maître D': Sir, please relax. Rudy will wait as long as need be, huh.
Rudy: Yeah, you relax and let your ass do the talking.
Maître D': Rudy!
The Maître D' makes a signal for Rudy to be quiet.
The man looks at him and uncomfortably answers.
Man: So um. Yeah, my parents can't wait to meet you, too.

Woman: How's the duck?
Man: Uh I bet it's good.
The man FARTS and Rudy backs and sits up smiling.
Rudy: (smiling, amused) Hey, speaking of ducks, I hear something quackin'!
Maître D': Rudy, please!
Man: So, uh, you better be careful or my mom's gonna bore you with her garden stories.
Woman: Thanks for the advanced warning.
Rudy: Hey, there, general, have you deployed any troops yet?
Maître D': Rudy!

It's often said that emotion is a drug, and in comedy, we just say no. That's actually not true. But what is true is that only one person in a scenario can have the emotional focus at any one moment. It's clear that in this sketch, the character we care about, even as we're laughing at him and with him is David Cross. You could certainly shift the focus any time to the girl, or Rudy, or even the Maître D', but only one at a time.

The man makes a face as he is going poop in the box.
Rudy: Hey! Now that's what I'm talkin' about! You folks have a good evening.
Man: (to the Maître D') Do you have any toilet paper?
Maître D': Eh, shh, shh, shh, we do not have something as crude as a toilet paper. (claps) FRENCHY!
A man dressed like a chimney sweep comes out of the back room with a cart full of cleaning supplies.
Frenchy: Hello, guv'ner! Well, no need to fumigate here this month!

OK, as Python would say, that's enough silliness. But how would straight line/ wavy line appear in a full-length narrative? While it wouldn't be as absurd or extreme as in a sketch, the dynamics are still the same, as you can see from the scene from *Meet the Parents*. Ben Stiller's character has just left his fiancée's house in disgrace, and all he wants is to get on a plane, go home, and leave the whole mess behind him.

An airport terminal at the gate. Night. The place is empty, there is not one other passenger besides Greg Focker at the gate. The airline employee is the only other person there.
Greg walks up to the airline employee with his bag.
Airline employee: Oh hello.
She takes his boarding pass and looks at it.
Airline employee: I'm sorry, we're only boarding rows 9 and above right now, you'll have to wait.
She hands him back the pass.
Greg looks at the pass.

Greg: I'm in row 8.
Airline employee: Please step aside sir.
Greg: It's just one row, don't you think it's okay?
Airline employee: We'll call your row momentarily.
He stares at her, she stares back.
Airline employee: Step aside sir.
Shot inside terminal. No one is there and there is a man cleaning.
Greg looks around and then back at the employee.
He takes a couple steps back. She looks around, smiles and waits a few more moments.
Greg stares at her. She avoids his eyes, then finally picks up the pager phone and makes an announcement.
Airline employee: Thank you for waiting, we'd like to continue boarding the aircraft now. We're now boarding all rows now. All remaining rows.
She puts the page down, Greg walks up to her.
Airline employee: Um, hello.
She looks at the boarding pass and nods, smiling.
Airline employee: Enjoy your flight.
He grabs the pass and boards.

Now notice how few "jokes" there are in the scene, how little you have to write for this character. Why write puns or bon mots or epigrams for him? Why? What's the point? How would that help? Just let him deal with the situation. And when he needs to talk, let him say what you would say in that situation.

To sum up: the comedy is created by someone struggling (wavy line) against someone who's blind to the problem or creating the problem (straight line). Remember, there isn't always a straight line/wavy line dynamic in a scene, if the scene is expositional or dramatic in nature.

When acting a straight line, the focus should be on either creating obstacles for the wavy line or being blind or indifferent to the obstacles that are there. When playing a wavy line moment, the focus for the actor is to be vulnerable to everything in the environment (for instance, allow yourself to have multiple points of focus in the scene) but still lack the skills necessary to solve or make total sense of the problem.

No matter what the medium may be, whether the traditional theatre, the sketch or improv stage, television or film, the technique and the approach is the same. Whether it's a scene from *Rosencrantz and Guildenstern are Dead*, or *Everybody Loves Raymond*, or *Monty Python's Life of Brian*, the comedy is based on the moment-to-moment teamwork where one character is struggling to make sense of the sometimes illogical, baffling and disconcerting behaviors of the other characters in the scene. While the medium or audience may affect the attack and tone of the straight line character—broader in a sitcom, more subtle in Shaw and Shakespeare—the wavy line remains grounded in the performer's flawed and flailing humanity.

Straight line/wavy line is:

- The one who does not see and the one who does.
- The one blind to, or creating, the problem, and the one struggling with the problem.
- The essential dynamic of comic focus, not character.

Exercises

- Tape two or three episodes of a sitcom. Note who is playing a straight line and who is a wavy line at each moment in the scene.
- Read a contemporary comedy, like Neil Simon's *The Odd Couple*, Terrance McNally's *It's Only a Play*, or David Mamet's *Glengarry Glen Ross*. Mark who is the wavy line (who has our emotional focus) in each scene.
- Try the "Honey, I'm home" writing exercise below.

"Honey, I'm home"

I call this exercise "Honey, I'm home" after the timeless sitcom greeting. The object of the exercise is to write a two character, one-page scene that puts the two characters in a straight line/wavy line dynamic. For the purpose of this exercise, don't switch focus between the characters. Write one character as a straight line (blind to or creating the problem) and the other as the wavy line (struggling with the problem, but unable to solve it because the character's a non-hero.

An example would be:

He:	Honey, I'm home!
She:	Arrrggghhh!
He:	What?
She:	Avast ye landlubber! Arrrggghh!
He:	Why is there all this water in the kitchen?
She:	Arrrggghhh! You'll be walking the plank, ye will! Arrrgggh!
He:	*(Beat)* I have to tell you—I'm a little freaked out by that parrot.

It should be clear that he is a wavy line and she is a street-rat crazy straight line. You don't actually have to start with "Honey, I'm home!" but you're free to do so if the spirit moves you. Here are a few examples from recent classes:

Leonard:	What time is it? I have a date at seven with the new Physics professor and I don't want to be late.
Sheldon:	That depends. Do you mean Pacific, Mountain, Central, or Eastern time?

Leonard: Why would I plan a date for seven o'clock in another time zone?
Sheldon: Any number of reasons. All of the time zones have their advantages and disadvantages. Some areas of the Mountain Time Zone don't observe Daylight Savings Time, the Central Time Zone includes my wonderful home state of Texas, while the Eastern Time Zone is the first to experience the miracle of nightfall. Perhaps the Pacific Time Zone is the most convenient though, since we do live in it. But to answer your first question, it's seven-oh-five.
Leonard: Thanks, now I'm late for my date. In all four time zones.

Joe: Hot girl you're with tonight.
Dave: That's my sister.
Joe: I get it. Your "sister."
Dave: No, really.
Joe: It's cool man. I'm not going to tell Anna.
Dave: There's nothing to tell.
Joe: Exactly.
Dave: Stop winking at me!
Joe: Right. Don't want to give it away.
Joe elbows Dave in the ribs.
Dave: She. Is. My. Sister.
Joe: Dude. I got the cover story the first time.

A small airplane cockpit. Night. Mr. Straight line (pilot) and Mr. Wavy line (passenger) in mid-flight.
Pilot: What would you say if I told you I don't know how to fly?
Passenger: What?!
Pilot: Yeah, I can't fly. I have no idea what I'm doing.
Passenger: You're flying now. You're flying now and you're doing a great job.
Pilot: That's just your opinion.
Passenger: It's a fact! It's an actual fact!
Pilot: We're going to die.
Passenger: (shouting) WE'RE NOT GOING TO DIE!
Pilot: You need to remain calm, sir. I'm flying a plane.
Passenger: Please tell me you can land this thing.

In all three examples, it should be pretty easy to spot the wavy line—it's the character that isn't saying a lot, other than, "What?" In fact, "What?" is the perfect non-hero wavy line dialogue. It sees something, but it just doesn't quite know what it sees.

Elaine: Is that a hot dog?
Frank: Is that a metaphorical question?
Elaine: No.

Frank:　It's a compendium of condiments, a prodigious palace of protein—
　　　　(interrupted by his wife's glare). Too much alliteration?
Elaine:　No. Too many nitrates, organs and bones.
Frank:　Like those are bad things. Organs are high in iron and bones have
　　　　great calcium.
Elaine:　Try a soy dog. They were on sale.
Frank:　For a reason.
Elaine:　They're good for your heart.
Frank:　But they can't be good for my soul.

This example is cleverly written—and that's the problem with it as a "Honey, I'm home" exercise. Both characters are so verbal, so witty, so aware of each other that not only is there no struggle (there's just a difference of opinion, not the same thing) but it also represents a bit of "ping-pong" dialogue. Ping-pong dialogue is when characters bat words and phrases back and forth to each other. "Too much alliteration?" "Too many nitrates." "They're good for your heart." "They can't be good for my soul." Very Noël Coward, but unless you *are* Noël Coward, something to be avoided because for the most part, that's not the way people talk. Most people talk past one another "Honey, take out the garbage." "Uh, wait a minute, it's the 9th inning," or "Have you paid that bill? Gotta run!"

Acknowledgments

Reprinted from *Hidden Tools of Comedy* by Steven Kaplan, published by Michael Wiese Productions, www.mwp.com. The author gratefully acknowledges the invaluable help of Rhonda Hayter and my wife Kathrin King Segal, who saved me from my sins, grammatical and others; to the actors and artists of the Manhattan Punch Line Theater, where this concept, along with many others in my book, The Hidden Tools of Comedy, first emerged; and especially to Brad Bellamy, who told me I had to write it all down I-don't-want-to-admit-how-many years ago.

Notes

1　The scene below can be found at www.youtube.com/watch?v=WQXwt83hYkE.
2　In my book *The Hidden Tools of Comedy*, I use the term "non-hero" to describe someone who lacks some, if not all, the skills required in a situation. Sometimes the skill is intelligence, with a foolish character, or the skill lacking may be empathy or honesty in a rascally character. A lack of skills creates more potential, whereas possessing skills, such as sensitivity or comprehension, creates more of a dramatic moment.
3　The scene starts at 1:07 on this Vimeo link: http://vimeo.com/21291918.
4　The video is available on YouTube at www.youtube.com/watch?v=QKwJHblt63U, starting at 6:06.

References

Belz, Aaron. 2007. "Something Mechanical Encrusted on the Living": The Influence of Popular Comedy on Modern American Poetry, 1900–1960. Dissertation, Saint Louis University. Ann Arbor: UMI. ATT 3280178.

Bergson, Henri. 1956. "Laughter." In Wylie Sypher (ed.), *Comedy*. Baltimore, MD: Johns Hopkins University Press, pp. 59–190.

Glienna, Greg, Mary Ruth Clarke, Jin Herzfeld and John Hamburg (2000) *Meet the Parents*. Universal.

Goldman, William. 2000. *Which Lie Did I Tell? More Adventures in the Screen Trade*. New York: Pantheon.

Kaplan, Steve. 2013. *The Hidden Tools of Comedy: The Serious Business of Being Funny*. Studio City, CA: Michael Wiese.

Koren, Steve. 1996. "The Abstinence." *Seinfeld*, season 8, episode 9, November 21. NBC.

Odenkirk, Bob and David Cross. 1998. "Rudy Will Await Your Foundation—The Burgundy Loaf." *Mr. Show*, season 4, episode 4. 16 November. HBO.

Wieck, David Thoreau. 1967. "Funny Things." *Journal of Aesthetics and Art Criticism* 25(4): 437–47.

3

USING PUNCTUATION TO FACILITATE COMEDY IN THE PLAYS OF GEORGE BERNARD SHAW AND BEYOND

Candice Brown

> When a thing is funny, search it carefully for a hidden truth.
> (George Bernard Shaw, *Back to Methuselah*)

The plays of George Bernard Shaw are widely celebrated for their pointed wit devoted to the exploration of social, political, and moral reform. A successful production immerses the audience in a heady mix of incisive argument and entertainment, and actors must have sophisticated skills to successfully unleash the comedy. Not only must the actor be able to fully embrace and master his character's intellectual argument, he must also be able to dance these mental steps within the strictures of Victorian decorum, and hopefully, harness the entertainment value of the inherent comedy along the way.

In my work as an acting and voice teacher, I use the plays of Shaw to challenge my upper level undergraduate and graduate musical theater acting students to fully inhabit these plays of ideas, and to find, explore, and illuminate their inherent comedy. One of the chief techniques I use is to work with them to recognize, explore, and apply a concept I refer to as Intrinsic Shavian Cadence (ISC). The following discourse will expound on the basic tenets of this technique, how I use it in a pedagogical setting, and how the training tends to inform student rehearsal and performance work.

In brief, the concept of ISC translates the elements of punctuation that shape Shaw's written dramatic lines into quantifiable elements of metrical time. When an actor accepts this suggested codification, the written punctuation becomes concrete and "playable" elements of rhythm, functioning in the same way that rest stops of different lengths do in written sheet music.

Written punctuation is an essential component of any authors craft, and there are countless examples of writers who use punctuation—sometimes strictly, sometimes willfully—to great effect: William Faulkner, ee cummings, David

Mamet, and of course George Bernard Shaw. An author's use of punctuation is *intrinsic* to any well-written text, each mark chosen consciously to clarify meaning for the reader. In a play script, the playwright depends on the actor to make his meaning clear to the audience. In this sense, I believe a playwright's chosen punctuation becomes even more important. They become vital suggestive clues from the playwright on how to craft the rhythm, or *cadence*, of the character's utterances. It's important to hear the sounds of words, but just as important to listen to rhythm of the silences between words. Punctuation informs rhythm, and rhythm helps drive the comic or dramatic action, speeding up or slowing it down to tell the story to its greatest effect. Cadence (inspired by punctuation) can reveal character, and tickle the audience's ears, especially in comedy.

Skilled actors openly acknowledge the value of analyzing cadence when working on blank verse. Any good performance of Shakespeare begins with a detailed analysis of the meter, with particular attention given to any variations from standard iambic pentameter. These variations are often seen as providing useful "flags" for the performer, as if Shakespeare left performance clues within the structure of his poetry. I do not think it a stretch to suggest that George Bernard Shaw penned his punctuation as carefully as Shakespeare penned his meter, in the hopes that it would help the actor to fully realize the passionate, often comedic, intellectual banter which form the backbone of his plays.

Before I continue, allow me to give credit where credit is due. The technique of using the punctuation in a play as a guide for performance choices does not originate with me. This specific codification system of interpreting Shavian punctuation was passed down to me by Laura Anne Worthen during the third year of my graduate study at the University of Pittsburgh. Ms. Worthen was my voice teacher, and directed me in several Shaw scenes during my masters training. I have no original or primary source material for this technique, nor did I consider an approach to working with punctuation in a play prior to her handing this technique down to me. I have tried to find the true source of this technique, but to no avail. So, I view my work with this system as part of the great ongoing oral tradition of teaching—where knowledge is passed in the classroom from one generation of artists to the next, with each teacher adding his or her own insights and experience to the mix. Still, I would like to give a note of thanks to this teacher for introducing me to the importance of paying close attention to the punctuation in all plays. I had never conceived how important and valuable that attention could be or how it would illuminate my own understanding and exploration of text, not only the works of George Bernard Shaw, but also contemporary language driven plays. This devotion to punctuation has filled my professional life as a teacher and a performer with great insights and decades of laughter.

Shaw's plays are the ideal springboard for this technique because his plays of ideas present rich and complex intellectual banter in the context of a witty, sophisticated entertainment. How does the actor balance the two? How does he build and sustain the line of argument, never losing his intellectual grip, while milking each moment for comedy in order to keep the audience engaged, delighted, and amused?

This technique of ISC suggests that the answer is in the text itself, in the inherent structure created by Shaw's punctuation. When read aloud, Shaw's writing feels and sounds musical. The musical sound I refer to is revealed partly through the punctuation, which if noticed and played well, can offer many rhythmical opportunities for the actor that are often overlooked and generalized in performance. And, as Shaw's characters argue exhaustively about socio-economic, political, and feminist ideas, a facile playing of the punctuation can help the actor point up and illuminate those ideas while simultaneously underscoring the humor and wit so necessary to a successful production.

Now, let's jump right in and investigate how essential ideas are revealed to an actor by examining the punctuation in the plays of Shaw. Take a look at this selection from a scene between Julia and Charteris in act I of his play *The Philanderer*.

Julia, with a stifled cry of rage, rushes at Grace, who is crossing behind the sofa towards the door. As Grace exits, Charteris seizes Julia and prevents her from getting past the sofa.

Julia: *(Suddenly ceasing to struggle and speaking with the most pathetic dignity)* Oh, there is no need to be violent.

Charteris passes her across to the left end of the sofa, and leans against the right end, panting and mopping his forehead.

Julia: That is worthy of you!—to use brute force—to humiliate me before her! *(She breaks down and bursts into tears.)*

Charteris: *(To himself with melancholy conviction)* This is going to be a cheerful evening. Now patience, patience, patience! *(Sits on a chair near the round table.)*

Julia: *(In anguish)* Leonard, have you no feeling for me?

Charteris: Only an intense desire to get you safely out of this.

Julia: *(Fiercely)* I am not going to stir.

Charteris: *(Wearily)* Well, well. *(Heaves a long sigh.)*

They sit silent for a while, Julia struggling, not to regain her self-control, but to maintain her rate at boiling point.

Julia: *(Rising suddenly)* I am going to speak to that woman.

Charteris: *(Jumping up)* No, no. Hang it, Julia, don't let's have another wrestling match. I have the strength, but not the wind: you're too young for me. Sit down or else let me take you home. Suppose her father comes in.

Julia: I don't care. It rests with you. I am ready to go if she will give you up: until then I stay. Those are my terms: you owe me that—

Julia sits down determinedly. Charteris looks at her for a moment; then, making up his mind, goes resolutely to the couch, sits down near the right hand end of it, she being at the left; and says with biting emphasis.

Charteris: I owe you just exactly nothing.
Julia: *(Reproachfully)* Nothing! You can look me in the face and say that? Oh, Leonard!

The previous sample is a perfect example of two Shavian characters arguing passionately for their point of view. Now, let's look at Shaw's use of punctuation in the scene, using the codification system I alluded to earlier, which I call ISC. I've used this method for 23 years in the classroom, and I am amazed at how this simple technique helps actors to easily communicate the essential ideas of the scene, while effortlessly revealing the inherent comedy. The technique first asks the actor to recognize patterns and rhythmical beats assigned to the punctuation marks. This awareness will assist the playing of the comedy and help underscore and emphasize points within the argument between the characters.

Before I apply the technique to *The Philanderer* scene it may be helpful to expand on the ISC technique, and how to use it. First a measurable length is assigned to punctuation marks. You may compare it to the basic structure of music as a reference. If you look at a musical score you will notice many things about it: time signature, the key for which it is written, the length of each note, and so on. If you are about to learn to play or sing that piece of music, you would also notice where there are moments of silence or where to pause and for how long. Similarly, the ISC approach assigns punctuation markings a numeric value for length of silence. As a whole note in music receives a count of four, a half note, receives a count of two; a quarter note receives a count of one; so does a whole rest receive a count of four, a half rest a count of two and a quarter rest a count of one (see Figure 3.1).

Similarly, when observing ISC, a period will be held for a count of three, a colon or a semi-colon will be held for a count of two. A question mark or an exclamation mark will have no hold at all: the actor/character would continue straight on with the text either within a line or while picking up the cue for their next line. The cadence looks like this:

- comma (,) =1 beats/counts
- semi-colon and colon (;:) = 2 beats/counts
- period (.) = 3 beats/counts
- question mark and exclamation point (?!) = no beat (carry ON!)
- ellipsis (…) = 1 beat
- dashes (–) = 1, 2 or more beats.

Regarding the last item, the delineation for a dash or double dash is not absolutely defined, but proportional in duration to other beat values. In other words, you have flexibility with the counts given to the dashes depending on the weight of the moment in the scene or monologue. You will see the double dash used very specifically and frequently in Shaw's writing.

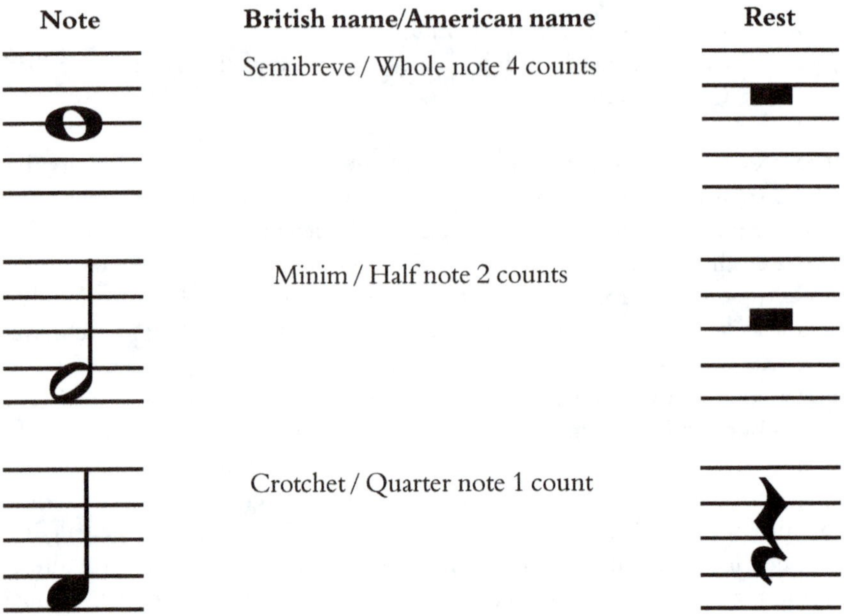

Note	British name/American name	Rest
	Semibreve / Whole note 4 counts	
	Minim / Half note 2 counts	
	Crotchet / Quarter note 1 count	

FIGURE 3.1 Notes and rests in music

Note and *rest* values are not absolutely defined, but are proportional in duration to all other note and rest values. The whole note is the reference value, and the other notes are named (in American usage) in comparison (i.e., a quarter note is a quarter the length of a whole note).

Let's return to our example between Charteris and Julia in Shaw's *The Philanderer*, this time with the ISC notated in the body of the scene. Try tapping along with a pencil as you read. Assign a brisk tempo to your tapping as you read. I have indicated the beats of the cadence in parenthesis. I have also removed the stage directions so they do not distract from or impede the flow of observing the cadence. I don't suggest or recommend the actors ignore the stage directions or eliminate them from the process of research for a scene, since Shaw's stage directions are pointed and deliberate, so to remove them entirely would be a grave mistake. Rather, I suggest that actors delete them from one version of their working script, to facilitate the learning of the cadence in this part of the rehearsal process.

Julia: Oh, **(1)** there is no need to be violent. **(3)** That is worthy of you! — **(0)** *(but then Shaw adds a double dash for **(1 or 2)**)* to use brute force — **(1 or 2)** to humiliate me before her! **(0)**

Charteris: This is going to be a cheerful evening. **(3)** Now patience, **(1)** patience, **(1)** patience! **(0)**

Julia: Leonard, **(1)** have you no feeling for me? **(0)**

Charteris: Only an intense desire to get you safely out of this. **(3)**

Julia: I am not going to stir. **(3)**

Charteris: Well, **(1)** well. **(3)**

Julia: I am going to speak to that woman. **(3)**

Charteris: No, **(1)** no. **(3)** Hang it, **(1)** Julia, **(1)** don't let's have another wrestling match. **(3)** I have the strength, **(1)** but not the wind: **(2)** you're too young for me. **(3)** Sit down or else let me take you home. **(3)** Suppose her father comes in. **(3)**

Julia: I don't care. **(3)** It rests with you. **(3)** I am ready to go if she will give you up: **(2)** until then I stay. **(3)** Those are my terms: **(2)** you owe me that, – **(1 or 2)** *(in this instance I prefer **(1)** to prompt Charteris's immediate reply and underline the sharpness of the tempo comedy).*

Charteris: I owe you just exactly nothing. **(3)**

Julia: Nothing! **(0)** You can look me in the face and say that? **(0)** Oh, **(1)** Leonard! **(0)**

And now, follow along in the next example and observe that even in more dramatic moments like in the final act of Shaw's *Mrs. Warren's Profession* the punctuation will help to move the intentions and point-of-view forward. Try tapping along again as you read. I have indicated the beats in parenthesis.

Vivie: Wait a moment: **(2 beats)** I've not done. **(3)** Tell me why you continue your business now that you are independent of it. **(3)** Your sister, **(1)** you told me, **(1)** has left all that behind her. **(3)** Why don't you do the same? **(No beat)** *(Immediate cue pick up is illustrated here with no beat after Vivie's question at the end of her line. Mrs. Warren giving way to her "listening objective," or what she is listening for ... The actor and audience are meant to learn that the character of Mrs. Warren has heard all she needs to hear even before Vivie poses the final question ...)*

Mrs Warren: Oh, **(1)** it's all very easy for Liz: **(2)** she likes good society, **(1)** and has the air of being a lady. **(3)** Imagine me in a cathedral town! **(No beat)** *(underscoring perhaps the indignation and the absurdity of the idea)* ... Why, **(1)** the very rooks in the trees would find me out even if I could stand the dullness of it. **(3)** I must have work and excitement, **(1)** or I should go melancholy mad. **(3)** And what else is there for me to do? **(0)** The life suits me: **(2)** I'm fit for it and not for anything else. **(3)** If I didn't do it somebody else would; **(2)** so I don't do any real harm by it. **(3)** And, **(1)** then it brings in money; **(2)** and I like making money. **(3)** No: **(2)** it's no use: **(2)** I can't give it up—**(1 or 2)** not for anybody. **(3)** But what need you know about it? **(No beat)**—*(again she isn't really waiting for an answer. The fact that her line continues is proof.)* I'll never mention it. **(3)** I'll keep Crofts away. **(3)** I'll not trouble you much: **(2)** You see I have to be constantly running about from one place to another. **(3)** You'll be quit of me altogether when I die. **(3)**

Notice how the cadence in both examples gives the actor a rhythm to follow which facilitates the way the idea is perceived by the audience. It's a useful clue for playing, breathing, and handing off text. Once in rehearsal, you will immediately sense and hear how masterful the punctuation works with the rhythm of the British dialect used in Shaw's plays to underline his character's point of view, articulate the language and facilitate quick breath intake for the actor. Even though there are dialectical variants written in some of Shaw's characters it doesn't alter the landscape for the punctuation. For example: the Cockney dialect Eliza uses in *Pygmalion* or other characters such as the chocolate loving Swiss mercenary soldier in *Arms and the Man*. We can assume that Shaw's environment growing up and Irish culture did influence the playwright and that Shaw certainly was writing with an ear towards the British dialect with his roots grounded solidly in his Irish upbringing. However in this instance both the Irish dialect and the British dialect are neighbors and have similar musical rhythms. And, whether a play is directed with or without a British dialect, or any other, the observance of punctuation and attention to cadence still proves useful.

Here is how to explore the punctuation with actors in rehearsal.

Enlarge a copy of the ISC so that a copy of it can be placed on a music stand beside the script as the actors begin to learn how to incorporate it. The punctuation can then be tapped out by someone while the scene is read and worked by the actors. A drum stick on a block of wood or a conductor's baton works well with a music stand. Even a pencil works well as a tool for tapping on a desk or a table. Designate an actor who is not acting in the scene to do the tapping of the rhythm so that they will become familiar with it for use on their own scene when it's their turn to rehearse and also so those who are reading or performing/blocking/working/observing will be able to simply listen to the cadence and be mindful of it as an undercurrent reminding them of the punctuation as the rehearsal progresses.

When the actors tap for one another in a scene or monologue, they begin to feel the punctuation in their bodies in a kinesthetic way so it's really two ways of learning the beats; one as actor and another as tapper/facilitator. It's a good idea to have the tapper stand and use the whole body while they tap for a richer experiential learning process. The beats or rests then become memorized in the body's muscle memory as well as the memory of the mind just like the text of the scene gets memorized by listening, speaking and doing. I have worked with actors who are also tap dancers and they have commented on how much fun this process would be using their tap shoes to tap out the cadence of the punctuation.

Once you have selected a scene or monologue and have the ISC to follow beside you, it's a good idea to think about tempo. Like any piece of music, tempo will vary depending on the music. In this technique it's helpful, if you are tapping, to establish a brisk pace but not one that feels too fast for the actors rehearsing the scene. Resist moving immediately into *allegro* (fast) or the actors will become frustrated. It's fine to push the tempo but keep it moderate at the beginning of rehearsals for everyone to learn the cadence along with the thoughts and point of view of the characters.

An immediate cue pick-up as indicated with a question mark or an exclamation point is not necessarily an indicator of speed. These are different concepts. It may be helpful to think of it like this: Early rehearsals for an actor are like that of a musician or a dancer. The actor will break their process down and learn the punctuation as they learn their lines and the points of the story they are telling just like the musician first learns the notes before singing the entire song and the dancer learns the steps of the choreography before putting them together and creating an entire dance. In all of these examples speed will come into play later. The same is true for an actor using the ISC. The actor should think of speed later in the process. It becomes fun and challenging for the actor to pick up the pace in the scene or monologue, and can assist the comedy but all things in good time.

Let's look at a cut from another comedy by Bernard Shaw. This selection is from *You Never Can Tell*. In this comic scene of seduction follow along with the punctuation and notice how rich it is with comic opportunities. Especially in the places that have **(0)** beats marked to rest. Tap along as you read.

Gloria: *(Uneasily, rising)* Let us go back to the beach. **(3)**
Valentine: *(Darkly– – –looking up at her)* What! **(0)** you feel it, **(1)** too? **(0)**
Gloria: Feel What? **(0)**
Valentine: Dread **(0)**
Gloria: Dread! **(0)**
Valentine: As if something were going to happen. **(3)** It came over me suddenly just before you proposed that we should run away to the others. **(3)**
Gloria: *(Amazed)* That's strange– – –**(1–3)** very strange! **(0)** I had the same presentiment. **(3)**
Valentine: How extraordinary! **(0)** *(Rising)* Well: **(2)** shall we run away?
Gloria: Run away! **(0)** Oh, **(1)** no: **(2)**

ISC helps actors understand that punctuation is filled with all sorts of acting opportunities. The elimination of a pause can add variety and be very effective for moving the action and adding a sense of urgency in a scene of a play especially for the audience. Of course this cadence technique is used as an exploratory exercise in the rehearsal process. It is used while digging into the essence of language as well as into the rhythms inherent in comedic and dramatic plays. It's not meant to supplant an actor's own spontaneity, intuition, or personalized rhythmic interpretations of a line. It is meant to inform, lift out, reveal and be another opportunity for discovery.

Once you have the ISC and your lines memorized and feel confident that all is going along well with acting intentions in the scene or monologue, the next step can be to use the technique to inspire blocking choices and offer opportunities for physical and vocal variation. Improvisation in rehearsal is a good companion tool to help with this part of the process.

One improvisation I've had success with in comedic scene work especially is to change direction (through movement and varied vocal pitch) at every new thought in a line of text, as indicated by the punctuation. It's a simple enough beginning point, and because the goal is to explore for new inspirations, where you physically end up in the room (or on stage) is of little consequence. The physical movement will underscore a new thought and also add fullness to the impulse of breath and variety to the voice. It can be useful to try more poetical or grander gestures with the punctuation and extreme pitch fluctuations at the same time. I find using this kind of improvisation helps the actor to have confidence and begin to work more broadly and musically with the text, breath, body, and voice. I suggest movements as physically challenging as diving onto the floor or pretending to sword fight. Then, see if this reveals anything about an opportunity for the character to advance or retreat with an imaginary sword. I encourage jumping up on chairs at an exclamation point, or throwing balls at a scene partner at a question mark, closing a door at a period, clapping on a comma, stomping twice on a colon or a dash. Although seemingly arbitrary, these explorations really start to engage the body with the mind, using the punctuation as a springboard.

It's important to keep the dialogue going as best you can while trying all sorts of new things. If scripts are still in hand you can absolutely begin this next step by simply changing direction when walking or sitting, standing, etc., in response to the ISC. Then, as you add the physicality into the timing of the cadence you will notice the size of the breath increasing and the musicality of the voice will also start to deepen and layer in here. As you continue to introduce movement try also coming in on a different pitch than your scene partner or the last actor went out on. Deliberately beginning your line using all the colors available in the voice to help achieve the points you'd like to underscore in the argument or text. Make your points stand out brightly with the use of the ISC.

As you can see there is a lot that can be explored with this work. It's variations can be as complex or as simple as you like. But, it is important to take one step at a time. Don't add too much too soon or all at once. You may be saying to yourself, "I can't possibly concentrate on all this at once!" Good! Concentrate on one aspect of the work each time through and then two, then, three, until you have it all going for you at once. For example, first *only* read the lines of the scene while tapping out the punctuation. Listen, respond and get the sense of the ISC. Next, memorize the scene while tapping out the punctuation and let the rhythms help inform you in making character choices to lift out point of view. Then, get up on your feet and allow this rhythm and the cadence to influence big physical choices.

How an actor and director work in rehearsal is unique to each production and exploration. It's very possible to examine a scene or a monologue by concentrating first on dialect sound shifts or vocal scoring for pitch opportunities, length of vowels or consonant action that may connect to character intention. Some directors or actors might like to spend some time at the table discussing themes and story points, concepts, etc., But, at some point the actor will need to look at the lines for the purpose of memorization. It is helpful to do this part of the work as the scene is being tapped out. Then, rehearse the scene for accuracy with the ISC. Continue on and add in the physical play and improvisations to notice what is revealed. Remember *speed is the cherry on top*. Save going fast for last and remember rehearsals are for trying out new impressions and discoveries, isolating what makes the world of the play come to life. You will find many opportunities to illuminate your scene, monologue or production.

While using the ISC when working with actors over the years, especially those in the field of musical theater, I find they become very adept very quickly at multitasking. And, even though they think they might be working on one component of the ISC or dialect or blocking, they begin to be very proficient at doing many things quickly and all at once.

Let's return to a portion of the previous Shaw scene from *The Philanderer* between Charteris and Julia. Read along and imagine how much fun rehearsals become. In this example, I've indicated the ISC, movement suggestions and pitch shifts to support ideas in the argument. I've also included Shaw's stage directions which are numerous but very helpful (Shaw's stage directions appear without bold; my suggestions for physical gestures in **bold**).

Julia, with a stifled cry of rage, rushes at Grace, who is crossing behind the sofa towards the door. Charteris seizes her and prevents her from getting past the sofa, **throwing her over his shoulder***.*

Julia: *(Suddenly ceasing to struggle and speaking with the most pathetic dignity,* **as he sets her back on her feet***)* Oh, **(1)** there is no need to be violent. **(3) Adjusts her clothing** *(He passes her across to the left end of the sofa, and leans against the right end, panting and mopping his forehead)* **New pitch** That is worthy of you!—**(2) Straightens her hat** to use brute force—**(2) Pouting** to humiliate me before her! *(She breaks down and bursts into tears)*

Charteris: *(To himself with melancholy conviction)* **(0) (Replacing his hanky in his pocket)** This is going to be a cheerful evening. **(3) Checking his pocket watch. New pitch** Now patience, patience, patience! *(Sits on a chair near the round table)* **(0) Shaw gives the actor the stage direction to sit for the physical...but you could as easily choose something else more active...go to the window to check for Graces father, get a drink, etc.**

Julia: *(In anguish)* **New pitch** Leonard, **(1) New pitch** have you no feeling for me?

Charteris: **(no beat) New pitch and cross to get her to the door** Only an intense desire to get you safely out of this.

Julia: *(Fiercely)* **(3) Holds on to the sofa—New pitch** I am not going to stir.

It's very exciting to observe actors as they become adept at delivering the charged wit within Shaw's comedy in a bold way, become physically and vocally facile, and very, very funny.

Some final thoughts. Be sure to allow some flexibility for variety. Don't be imprisoned by the use of ISC with punctuation; for example, the double dash symbol which Shaw uses frequently, can have three beats, or one. As always, allow your own instincts about the ideas being argued, or production you are working on, to guide your choices in the end. The ISC and other suggestions offered in this chapter are only a technique designed to help you *reveal* what the comedy *might be* as you attune yourself to the text's potential rhythms. The codified beats of ISC can be a useful guide, but like most theories or patterns in language, should not be seen as an absolute rule to follow. For example, deliberately setting a pattern so well that the audience begins to expect it can be hilarious when, at the right moment, an unexpected departure is made. The director and the actors can use ISC as way to locate, explore and to reveal the inherent comedy in Shaw's plays, and to make the ideas given by the playwright jump off the page and fire out of the actor's mouth with dexterity and a well-tested point of view. So, I encourage you to search carefully for the hidden truths in Shaw's punctuation: if explored with fearless curiosity, they will help you master Shaw's pointed wit and sophisticated comedy.

Acknowledgments

I would like give special thanks to The Society of Authors, on behalf of the Bernard Shaw Estate; Mark Medoff for guidance and continuous enthusiastic support; Christopher Olson, Bryn Austin, Evan Haas, Adrianne Krstansky; and my family, Robert Hurley, Tucker, and Charlie for your love, support, and endless patience.

4

COMEDY THROUGH *COMMEDIA*

Judith Chaffee

> The sixteenth century represents the summit in the history of laughter.
>
> (Bakhtin 1984: 101)

> Laughter is a reflex … Humor is the only domain of creative activity where a stimulus on a high level of complexity produces a massive and sharply defined response on the level of physiological reflexes.
>
> (Koestler 1964: 31)

Ancient Greek and Roman actors knew that humor was a way to illuminate universal truths of human vulnerabilities and societal conditions: make an audience laugh and they will listen to what you say. Renaissance actors knew this well, and developed their theatre of *commedia all'improvissa* to reveal circumstances of master–servant relationships, love predicaments, and vagaries of power. Whether it is satire, physical play, verbal wit, improvisations, character impersonations, absurd or alternative situations, the actors who played with life as they saw it, creating situations to make audiences laugh, had the masses—rich and poor—in the palms of their hands.

Commedia all'improvissa later became known as *commedia dell'arte*, literally "comedy of the actors guilds." It began in sixteenth-century Italy, emerging from Renaissance recognition of ancient cultures through contemporary interpretations of popular rituals and entertainment. Angelo Beolco, in the early 1500s caught the attention of Venetian aristocrats with his clever and entertaining comedies, and in 1545, a group of actors signed an official contract of agreement to share their earnings. Thus the first comedy troupes were formed, ensuring professional commitment to quality entertainment.

Commedia dell'arte was, and is, comedy at its best: physical, improvisational, and situational, challenging performers to be quick-witted and physically connected to every moment. The skills for playing *commedia dell'arte* are essential skills for actors and comediennes today. The actors had to be quick-witted since the dialogue was primarily improvised. They needed skills of articulation both vocally and physically because they wore half masks representing stock characters, necessitating physical characterizations of societal archetypes. They needed moment-to-moment readiness to change course or take advantage of mistakes. They often performed in large, distracting spaces such as ducal palaces, piazzas and town centers, or outdoor festivals. They were rarely guaranteed an audience's attention; they had to earn it, often by including songs, dances, acrobatics, and juggling. The performers were talented and intelligent actors, singers, musicians, and dancers, and they needed skills of physical transformation and the ability to adapt to the vagaries of the audience.

> Plainly the knowledge of all the tricks of the trade in the world could never of itself be sufficient if the actor did not also possess the innate flair and that one gift indispensable for improvisation—the talent for giving time and time again the impression that he was saying something completely new, something which had just come into his head that very moment.
>
> (Fo 1991: 11)

Acquiring skills to promote readiness for spontaneity, audience awareness, "clown" vulnerability, physical and vocal character transformation, and universal "laws" of comic action are part of training for *commedia* and apply to the comic actor. Each of the exercises below will address these basic skills, and create awareness for transferring these skills to any style of acting comedy.

The body is the mask

Much like a red-nose mask (the world's smallest mask?), the masks of *commedia* reveal rather than conceal. This means that when an actor puts on a "nose" or other mask, the mask allows freedom in the whole body. Time and again, actors will claim how nervous they are to approach the moment in front of the audience, but putting on the red-nose or half mask allows a transformation from "this is about me trying to be funny" to "this is universally silly—I can do anything now."

Actor readiness: breathing easily and naturally.

We know from experience that true humor happens in the release of tension. Holding one's breath produces tension so that actions, presence, vulnerability, and spontaneity are stymied. An exhalation is basic upon entering a space but it is amazing how often a young comedian will not be aware of the breath he or she is holding. The exercise below is taught by Avner Eisenberg (Avner the Eccentric) at Celebration Barn in South Paris, ME. This exercise is the most basic and honest place to begin learning to be present and in the moment.

Exercise

The objective is to enter the space, see the audience, perhaps recognize in the moment something that is happening, and then find a reason to exit.

- *Process:* Inhale a breath on seeing the audience ("Taking them in"). Exhale fully on recognizing them, make eye contact with one or two individuals in the audience, notice a detail—such as someone has a shirt the same color, someone smiles at you, someone is fidgeting—and allow a small reaction or two. Then look at the exit, look at the audience, go toward the exit, and look at the audience one more time before leaving.
- *Coaching:* The most difficult moment is initially taking the breath and letting it release. The entrance can be repeated as often as needs be to make sure the release of breath is genuine. To understand this breath, consider arriving at the top of a beautiful mountain after a long hike, taking in the glorious view, and breathing a sigh of relief that you made it. The performer may enter with excess tension, unknowingly making fist, or fidgeting with clothing, or shifting weight back and forth. This can be a magical moment: perhaps something secret is being held in the hand if the performer is clenching a fist; or if the student is shifting from side to side nervously, maybe the shifting means purposely practicing a little dance? Could they embellish these?

This exercise works especially well with a red nose. It is helpful to set up the space with clear entrances and exits.

Spotting: being clear and precise with focus

Trying to be funny is rarely funny. Humor or comedy is a creative process that involves a dramatic, vulnerable, or logical situation that suddenly takes a surprising detour. Or it is a dramatic, vulnerable, or seemingly logical action in ridiculous circumstances. But to the comedic actor it is serious and logical—what we can call clown logic. Arthur Koestler describes a clever joke that is both unexpected and perfectly logical for the joke teller, but not normally logical for the situation:

> Camfort tells a story of a Marquis at the court of Louis XIV who, on entering his wife's boudoir and finding her in the arms of a Bishop, walked calmly to the window and went through the motions of blessing the people in the street. "What are you doing?" cried the anguished wife.
>
> "Monseigneur is performing my functions," replied the Marquis, "So I am performing his."
>
> Tension mounts as the story progresses but it never reaches its expected climax. The ascending curve is brought to an abrupt end by the Marquis' unexpected reaction, which debunks our dramatic expectations; it comes

like a bolt out of the blue, which, so to speak, decapitates the logical development of the situation. The narrative acted as a channel directing the flow of emotions; when the channel is punctured the emotion gushes out like a liquid through a burst pipe; the tension is suddenly relieved and exploded in laughter.

(Koestler 1964: 33)

Seriousness of purpose is a comic actor's gold. The actor who can commit seriously, even urgently, to a moment or idea that might have two conflicting frames of reference, or a ludicrous incongruence, is the performer who will have the audience guffawing.

Sincerely looking at someone in the audience, a quick turn of the head to look at a scene partner or someone opposite in the audience, checking back in with the first person in the audience is called "spotting" and is the simplest exercise for clarifying focus, usually eliciting chuckles. In a mask, the whole face should turn, rather than just looking with the eyes. More simply, with or without a mask, look with your nose—turn your head.

An excellent example of this is in "Blue Man Group," a contemporary performance group of 3 non-speaking actors who use movement, technology, and percussion music while checking in with the audience to include them in moment-to-moment discoveries during scenarios—clearly demonstrating the effectiveness of spotting (Blue Man Group 2010). Also, a "double take" is a type of spotting.

Exercise 1

In a circle, one person begins by looking across the circle, then immediately looks to the person on the right. That person receives the look, looks across the circle to someone specific, and then looks to the right, continuing to pass the focus counterclockwise around the circle.

- *Process:* Looks should be quick, specific, and purposeful. Once the focus has gone around the circle, the direction can change and be improvised.
- *Coaching:* Encourage commitment and simplicity. Adding an attitude or emotional context diminishes the power of the simple act of looking. Timing is everything. The surprise is in the quick look, even though we already know where it is going.

Spotting is the way *commedia* actors know who is talking next, and when to enter the dialogue. Improvisations involving more than two people can fall flat if more than one person is talking or taking an action. When actors on stage look to the performer who is talking next, the audience knows to look there also.

FIGURE 4.1 Boston University seniors using "spotting" in commedia masks

Exercise 2

This is an exercise involves spotting with text, to include an audience and a partner.

- *Process:* One person looks at someone across the circle (like talking to the audience), and begins a story that has no ending. Before finishing a sentence, that person looks to the person on one side, who then looks out at the audience and finishes the sentence and continues the story, or starts a new one, but does not finish the sentence and instead looks at the next person, who then looks at the audience and picks up speaking, continuing around the circle.
- *Coaching:* Encourage story lines to be dropped and picked up again later. All story lines are said with commitment, seriousness, and specificity. Physical actions can be included but the talking is to the audience, the spotting is to the next person to speak .Length of story lines can vary dramatically.

Physical readiness

Actors are often told to relax and find ease; this can be disastrous. It is different from active attention without excess tension. An actor in improvised physical comedy must be ready for any change, any opportunity to connect with an audience that demands focused attention to details and moment-to-moment awareness. Actors in this kind of physical performance cannot relax; they must be forever attentive to every moment, but if they work with excess tension, their reactions will be delayed. It is a high state of performance energy. Again, the performers in Blue Man Group demonstrate this skill of heightened physical awareness that is astute and highly entertaining—the kind of physical attention necessary to perform *commedia* (Blue Man Group 2010).

There are several games for physical readiness that involve quick reactions, staying alert, and recognizing failures (always an asset for a comedic performer). The next two exercises have several layers of attention, demanding release of excess tension as the actions get more complicated. Both exercises are used in some variation by physical trainers all over the world, but these in particular were learned from Carlos Garcia Estevez, a *commedia* performer and teacher at the Lecoq School in Paris, France.

Exercise 1

This exercise involves ball tossing, changing places, and passing magic.

- *Process:* In a circle, one person begins passing a ball underhand across the circle, saying the receiver's name, and throwing when that person makes contact. Continue throwing the ball to different people across the circle, eventually adding another ball, and then a third ball. Continue with the ball throwing, and add winking across the circle at another person who does not have a ball at the moment, and the two people trade places in the circle. Continue with the ball throwing, and winking to trade places, and add a fancy belt or cloth—a magic cloth—that is passed around the circle with an air kiss.
- *Coaching:* Encourage actors to make eye contact, but not stop the action. Encourage letting go of a need to say "Sorry" when a ball is dropped; this takes time and focus out of the action. Remind actors to stay loose in their knees, and attentive in their bodies to allow for quick responses. They must keep track of the magic cloth since a ball will not be tossed to them while they are holding the cloth.

Exercise 2

This exercise is called "Zip zap" and is one variation of many similar sound and movement exercises.

- *Process:* Performers are in a circle. One person begins sending a clap directed to the person on the right while at the same time saying "zip." This gets passed around the circle, and can change direction. "Zap" is a directed clap to someone specific across the circle. "Diddelly-do" is a gesture of sweeping the arm up and over to the second person on either side, while saying "diddelly-do." "Freeza" is a gesture of throwing an imaginary Frisbee to

FIGURE 4.2 Boston University senior acting majors playing ball tossing, winking and changing places

the third person on either side. "Boing" is a gesture of throwing the chest forward while saying "boing" to bounce the sound and movement back to the sender. When anyone errs (says zip for a zap, or misses a boing, etc.) they stop the action by repeating three times their reaction to making the mistake, and then they send a sound and movement to continue the play.

- *Coaching:* Speed is important but not at the expense of making eye contact. Continual reminders to stay alert in the body (like a shortstop in baseball waiting for the pitch, or basketball players lined up for a free throw, or a panther about to run for an antelope) The three repeats of the reaction to a mistake should each have the intensity and intent of the actual reaction.

Mask readiness

Masks, while not crucial for performing *commedia dell'arte*, are certainly one of the most familiar and obvious aspects of *commedia*. Donning a mask demands that the physical life of the actor must coincide with the context of the mask, such that the whole body is said to be "the mask."

Commitment to one's physicality is key to fulfilling the mask. One of the most difficult challenges is making a strong physical choice and going with it. Often it is one distinct change that may seem restrictive but ultimately allows for greater play as characters interact with one another and the audience. As far as we know from literature and art, each of the *commedia dell'arte* characters had very distinctive qualities that varied only as each actor or actress made the character come to life through them. There are several approaches to discovering the body's "mask," but the simple exercises below are a start.

Walking and standing are basics of physical transformation. These can be done with or without masks.

Exercise 1

Walk around the room at an energized pace—a five on a scale of one to ten. Notice habits. Each exploration below should be done with serious intent and commitment. To best understand this exercise, refer to John Cleese's Ministry of Silly Walks on YouTube (www.youtube.com/watch?v=iV2ViNJFZC8).

- Process:
  o Take larger steps than normal. Keep the pace at a five.
  o Take smaller steps than normal.
  o Walk on the heels or balls of the feet only.
  o Change the rhythm of the walk.
  o Walk with legs rotated inward (pigeon-toed).
  o Walk with legs rotated outward.
  o Stop and stand in a wider or narrower stance.
  o Stop and stand with toes turned in or out.
- Coaching:
  o Allow the arms to change with the changes in the walk.
  o Notice how the focus changes and exaggerate it.
  o Allow sounds in the walking and/or stopping.
  o Clarify your exaggerated walk and walk with someone else, having conversation.

Exercise 2

This exercise is called "animal movements." Most characters of *commedia dell'arte* are associated with particular animal types. Il Capitano, the warrior, can find his physicality in a bloodhound, or mastiff. Pantalone, the miser, has been described as a turkey or hen. Arlecchino, the lowly servant, could be a cat or monkey; il Dottore, the doctor, is a pig, and the evil servant, Brighella, is half cat and half dog. When wearing the appropriate mask and taking on the animal qualities, the characters' distinct personalities emerge.

- *Process:* Choose an animal to imitate, and try to discover how it navigates the space, negotiates with other animals, eats, sleeps, and plays.
- *Coaching:* If the animal has four legs, how does it move on only two as an animal? What sounds does the animal make? If the animal transformed into a human form, but retained the quality of the animal, how does it walk, run, sit, sleep, communicate, or play?

FIGURE 4.3 Boston University senior actor taking larger steps to find a character

Exercise 3

This is "changing the spine." Whether the pelvis is tucked under, or tilted forward drastically alters how one uses the spine, and consequently how the head, arms, and legs react and alter one's presence.

- *Process:* Tilt the pelvis under (tucking). Allow changes in the head, arms, and legs. Play with instructions from Exercise 1. Tilt the pelvis forward (arching the lower back). Play with notes from Exercise 1 above.
- *Coaching:* Allow the chest to collapse or expand. Find a distinct place for the hands with each adjustment. Allow sounds.

Partner readiness

Exercise 1

This exercise is about basic entrances and exits, and it can be done with or without masks. Using the ideas of spotting and moment-to-moment commitment, this exercise encourages immediacy of play and attention to timing. Two actors behind a curtain (or standing mat or some kind of barrier), decide by "rock/paper/scissors" who will enter first and must then enter immediately. The object of play is never to leave the space empty of a person, and, initially, no two actors can be in the space at the same time. All entrances and exits are done with speed—no one can meander on or off.

- *Process:* One actor enters, sees the audience, looks to the exit (either side), looks to the audience, and exits. The other actor must enter immediately as the actor exits. They continue entering and exiting until either both are in the space at the same time, or the space is left empty, or one of them forgets to check with the audience.
- *Coaching:* Exits can get braver, such as jumping out of the space, and the next can jump in, etc. Eventually include speaking with the audience before exiting.

Exercise 2

This exercise involves entrances and exits of characters, building on Exercise 1 above.

- *Process:* Two actors, each enter from opposite sides, on his/her way to the opposite side. Each actor physicalizes a character and chooses an objective (why he/she is going toward the opposite exit) and gives it urgency. Both actors decide before they enter whether they are strangers, lovers, friends, enemies, neighbors, or relatives. Speaking should be out to the audience, looking at the partner turns the dialogue over to him/her. Each finds a way to continue the conversation and/or to make an exit.
- *Coaching:* Dialogue is out to the audience. Allow changes in physical and vocal choices.

Lazzi

A chapter on sixteenth-century comedy should certainly include mention of *"lazzi,"* the physical actions so iconic to *commedia dell'arte*. *Lazzi* are small moments of physical comedy, often not related to the story telling but highly entertaining. There are many rationales for the derivation of the term *lazzi*, the comic stage business that in early Italian handwritten scenarios were penned in particular spots throughout the manuscripts. One sees the word *l'azzo*, (the term for action is *"azioni"* or *"azzi'*) and knows that a physical action was to occur, or did occur, at that moment in the scenario.

This chapter will not attempt to describe various *lazzi*, such as a simple slipping on a banana peel or servants throwing food around in a frenzy to hide from a master. There are several excellent physical comedy books which describe a range of comic physical actions: Mel Gordon's small but ample *Lazzi*, full of *lazzi* for a variety of situations, as well as his additional *lazzi* contributions to the *Routledge Companion to Commedia dell'Arte*. Davis Robinson's fine *Physical Comedy Handbook* offers clear descriptions of exercises for playing physical comedy.

However, in playing physical comedy, there are two important generally acknowledged "rules" of comedy to consider: understanding that an audience sees everything, and the law of numbers: threes and elevens in particular. For the first, it is important to remember that there is no "fourth wall" in comedy. Comedy is a game that the audience and performer play together. But fantasy and reality overlap: "The player builds tension by creating an easily broken fantasy world, and then breaks that tension with the acknowledgement of the absurdities or contradictions in the creation of that fantasy" (Foley 2015: 179).

If the performer firmly believes that a sausage is a weapon, the audience comes along for the ride, allowing the performer to use his weapon and then take a bite in the end—we knew it was only a sausage. It is the commitment of the performer that brings the audience into the fantasy and then the performer brings them back to reality.

As for the law of numbers, three is the shortest number of times to repeat an action and then surprise the audience: the setup and then shattering the expectation. One actor is trying to move a "heavy" chair; he asks a strong looking partner to help. Together they cannot move the chair. A small woman comes in and lifts the chair (which was actually made of Styrofoam) and takes it offstage. This would be less successful with only one attempt to move the chair or might lose the surprise with more than two attempts to lift the "heavy" chair.

The law of elevens is essentially the opposite: repeat an action so many times—at least eleven—since anything less than that will not offer a surprise but rather meets the audience's expectations that the performer will eventually stop doing the action and change. But after nine or ten times, the audience cannot believe the performer is actually going to do it again, and thus laughter ensues. In repeating an action, each repetition should be slightly different than the preceding one, even in the law of threes. For example, a performer tries to set up a ladder, each time failing in some way but never in the same way, each attempt building on what the performer (and the audience) knows from the experience. In the law of elevens, a performer carries a glass of water while running across the space; next time he tries to take a drink while running but fails—each attempt at the entrances and exits enhances the possibilities of finally getting the drink (next time trying to pour the water from the glass into a water bottle, carrying a straw, then a towel, then a water pump, and so on until finally stopping to take a drink …

Commedia today

The primary characters of *commedia*—Arlecchino (Harlequin), the prankish servant; Columbina, the smart, female servant; Pantalone, the lascivious miser; La Signora, the rich diva; Dottore, who pompously professes to know everything; Capitano, the braggart coward; Innamorati, the young lovers; Brighella, the charming but evil innkeeper—can still be found in society today. Young Lovers are everywhere, preening to attract the opposite (or same) sex, often irrationally and naively. Professors, scientists, company heads, and especially politicians, reflect Dottore who loved to pontificate and march around as if what he was saying was of utmost importance. We all know boisterous, boastful intruders who will try anything to avoid difficult situations or confrontations (Capitano). Every town or neighborhood has its Pantalone, the older, wealthy resident who thinks he can get away with anything and has aches and pains that keep him complaining. The wise, patient schoolteachers, community helpers, and best friends are the Columbinas, who seem to know the truth of a situation and how to find solutions. And the most loved of all was Arlecchino (Harlequin) who represented the kid in us all: the eagerness for approval, the impulsive, often irrational, reactionary outbursts and continual search for something good to eat. Each of these character types lends potential for creating unpredictable, relevant, and humorous situations.

Commedia is situational comedy by actors making bold choices, physically and vocally. It is important to remember that *commedia dell'arte* means comedy of the actors, begun by performers who recognized what was happening in their changing world and used recognition of the social construct to create humor. Monty Python in the 1960s and the San Francisco Mime Troupe commented on social status, allowing us to laugh at those in power and the impossible situations they created. Audiences continue to be enchanted by the physical and vocal humor of situational comedy, such as *Fawlty Towers*, *Gilligan's Island*, and the Marx Brothers. These are examples in which the actors found physical and vocal qualities of likeable characters, consistently confronted in each episode by challenging and ridiculous circumstances, thus allowing an audience to laugh at their often-futile attempts to succeed.

Superseding the improvised text of Renaissance *commedia*, Carlo Goldoni, an Italian playwright of the eighteenth century, wrote *A Servant of Two Masters,* which has become one of the best examples of *commedia*'s style and wit. This play is one of the few iconic examples of *commedia* that still incites laughter and delight for contemporary audiences, as demonstrated by Christopher Bayes's 2013 Yale Repertory Theatre production that toured the US.

The relevance of *commedia* can be seen in productions of *Scapin* by Moliere, adapted by Jim Dale and Frank Dunlop in 1985 or as played by Bill Irwin at the Roundabout Theatre Company in 1996. In 2009, David Grimm premiered a *commedia dell'arte* play, *The Miracle at Naples*, at the Huntington Theatre Company in Boston; its premise was a roving *commedia* troupe setting up for performances in Naples while its players wittingly avoided work through complicated trysts and romps. More recently, Richard Bean adapted Goldoni's *A Servant of Two Masters* to *One Man, Two Guv'nors*, set in 1963 Brighton, England. It toured the US in 2012, winning over audiences on Broadway, and earning a Tony for its lead actor, James Corden.

Traditional *commedia dell'arte* may be too outdated to incite laughter from a contemporary audience, but certainly the elements of good humor have not changed. *Commedia* brought us a tradition of highly skilled performers breaking the fourth wall to entertain and enlighten an audience. While masks bring magic to clarifying characters, and physical actions bring comic relief, and improvising texts brings anticipation to the plot, it is the immediate creation of theatre on stage that encompasses the true splendor of comedy.

Considering *commedia* in the twenty-first century, the characters of *commedia* must be reflective of archetypes in societies throughout the world. Knowing this, the international Theatre Hotel Courage, directed by Katrien van Beurden of Netherlands, develops contemporary shows based on a form of modern *commedia dell'arte* in countries where people are living under challenging conditions. Actors trained in *commedia* learn to play extemporaneously, incorporating human foibles in the moment, on stage, affecting the performers and audiences alike with the universality of their masks and their needs. The audiences viewing these *commedia*-like performances seem to understand they are being taken into another realm of experience and having archetypical reactions (van Beurden 2015: 491):

> The Hotel Courage tour offers us authentic, beautiful, and funny stories from around the world told through the masks. The archetypal characters allow stories to transcend time, space and culture and reveal needs we all have in common, showing us a place where we can laugh and cry about how we try to survive in the world of today.
>
> (Van Beurden 2015: 496)

References

Bakhtin, Mikhail (1984) *Rabelais and His World*. Bloomington, IL: Indiana University Press.

Blue Man Group (2010) "Drumbone (Melodifestivalen 2010 Sweden)." See www.youtube.com/watch?v=dOLBn8GKBlA (accessed December 2014).

Chaffee, Judith and Oliver Crick (eds.) (2014) *Routledge Companion to Commedia dell'Arte*. Abingdon: Routledge

Cleese, John (1970) "Monty Python's Ministry of Silly Walks." See www.youtube.com/watch?v=iV2ViNJFZC8 (accessed December 2014).

Fo, Dario (1991) *The Tricks of the Trade*. New York: Routledge.

Foley, Brian (2015) "Principles of Comedy." In Judith Chaffee and Olly Crick (eds.), *Routledge Companion to Commedia dell'Arte*. Abingdon: Routledge.

Gordon, Mel (2001) *Lazzi: The Comic Routines of the Commedia dell'Arte*. New York: PAJ Publications.

Koestler, Arthur (1964) *The Act of Creation*. London: Hutchinson & Co.

Robinson, Davis (1999) *Physical Comedy Handbook*. Portsmouth, NH: Heinemann Drama.

Van Beurden, Katrien (2015) "Commedia in a New World Context." In Judith Chaffee and Olly Crick (eds.), *Routledge Companion to Commedia dell'Arte*. Abingdon: Routledge.

5

PHYSICALIZING FARCE

Davis Rider Robinson

Acting in farce requires a great respect for character motives, attention to individual rhythms, and ease and elasticity in blocking that allows action to flow unimpeded towards great comic collisions. That means actors who are fully engaged and physically alert. Farce also requires a sense of empathy and connection to the audience, as absurd as the motives of some of the characters may be. The thrill ride to the climax can only happen when the audience is interested in or cares about the players. While farcical writing usually involves clever plotting, it often draws characters in stereotypes. Actors need to ground their portrayals in something real and believable. Most great farces, though written primarily for entertainment value, have real human attributes actors can connect to. If it is a human weakness that has been taken to the extreme, actors need to identify with and amplify that foible. Find the humanity in a farce without slowing it down and it will be a much better show than one played strictly for laughs. Pre-planning on the part of the director and designers can make the journey easier, but the life of a farce is found in the casting and in the rehearsal hall. *Always*. The clever comeback or plot twist in one production can bring down the house, while in another theater the same play elicits no response whatsoever. The playing is all.

Great farcical writing does not act and direct itself; it can only be brought freshly to life in the playing, which isn't easy. Actors, directors, and designers must believe in the need for doing the show if they are to create a world that audiences will care about and enjoy. A sure-fire farce like Michael Frayn's *Noises Off* or Joseph Kesserling's *Arsenic and Old Lace* can be played so flatly or so frantically that audiences tune out. Misinterpretation can kill a well-written farce much faster than it can hurt a classical tragedy. The writing in a farce is "thinner" than a drama exploring deeper philosophical and psychological issues, so the players and director must be adept at keeping the soufflé alive. If they miss a beat, the wind goes out of a show's sails very quickly. Common errors are to make the production too frantic, too one-note, too "funny," too rigidly stylized, too selfish, too labored, too slow, or too under-rehearsed. Timing requires accuracy, which requires practice. Even highly skilled actors need time to fine-tune which millimeter and which microsecond to use with each beat. Everyone on stage needs to play vigorously with real truth and consequences and a sense of ease and grace, which means taking time to find the same, believable farce world. The more discoveries are made in rehearsal through play, the more likely the show will be a success. Of all genres, farce probably requires the least amount of "table work" (text analysis and dramaturgy around the table.) The sooner you get on your feet, the better.

Basics

A farce builds momentum from scene to scene as actors work methodically in pairs and trios to advance their agendas and create sub-plots that collide later in the play. These collision scenes are the hardest to do, so first start working on the small scenes that lead to these big events. What games are being played? Is it a one-upping scene? A battle of insults? A set-up for the person entering? A running gag? The function of each scene helps actors find the spine of their characters and defines the world of the play. The big door-slamming chase scenes farces are famous for will only work when these smaller units are well crafted. Otherwise, there is no momentum building up to the climax, and nothing to care about when all hell breaks loose. Later in this chapter I will discuss rehearsal tactics for shaping the small scenes and for staging some of the big ones.

One essential tactic is to schedule a frequent "All Call" for the whole cast to build vocabulary and esprit de corps, even if it is just for an hour. Later, this time slot can be used to block the big scenes and choreograph any staged mayhem. All Call is not a time to make friends with everyone. It is for actors to practice hitting and receiving the ball well together, like any good sports team. Practice making eye contact, listening to each other, and playing nimbly with verbal and physical cues found in the production. Farce is a team sport. Each character has its own rhythm and function in the plot, and actors need to find a unified playing style specific to the chemistry of their acting ensemble. Basic energy games and ensemble drills are a good place to start. Even something as simple as having everyone run and pause on a cue will help develop groupthink. Try devising games to play vigorously with the language and actions of the play. Some writers are darker and more acerbic than others; the energy of the cast and the mood in the rehearsal hall needs to channel the words of the playwright. All Call helps put actors into the same world.

The challenge of bringing small scenes together to a satisfying climax is usually the task of the director, who orchestrates the big picture with input from the actors. The playwright has crafted a roadmap for maximum comic

FIGURE 5.1 *You Can't Take It With You* (Jodi Bohan, Catherine Buscemi, Ben Jones, Brent Popolizio, Heather O'Brien, Jason Dugré, Cullen Sprague), Emerson College, 1995. Photographer: Davis Robinson

effect, built on many individual moving parts that need to function with vitality and honesty to lead up to the big chase scenes and final denouements. Before breaking down any individual scenes or talking about staging climactic finales, here are a few "big picture" rules that need stating.

1   *Do not try to be funny.* Most characters in farce are in horrible dilemmas they are trying to escape. They are often in miserable emotional states, and are doing their best to survive competing bad options. Farce requires the truthful playing of those needs just as much as with drama, except that the touch and tone of playing is a bit lighter and quicker. Trying to be funny means you aren't invested fully in your character's dilemma. Let the audience make up their own minds. In drama, a domestic argument can lead to violent and horrible consequences. Farcical arguments are equally passionate, but audiences know there will be no permanent damage to the relationship, so they laugh instead of cry.

2   *Be true to your rhythms.* Each character in a farce, like gears in a watch, moves to their own beat and must synchronize with the others to produce a functioning mechanism. Be aware of your function in the greater piece, but not absorbed in yourself. Every action impacts the other players on stage, and each actor needs to be alert to the impact they are having and react to that as well, including whether they are pushing a moment too far, too slow, need to prod more, etc.

3 *Play impulsively.* See above. Especially in a blocking rehearsal, directors and actors should look for where the "game" is, and go for it. Keep eyes and ears open for opportunity, and allow the body to fully react to all surprises and commit to all actions. You can always trim back on business if it gets too busy.

4 *Comedy floats, tragedy sinks.* Fight, but have fun in the fight. Worry and panic when appropriate, but do it with a joyous spirit, not one that has no pleasure. Be a wet blanket in the show if that is your role as a character (e.g. Malvolio), but enjoy doing it. Never flatten the playing. Despair in real life is draining; in a farce it is highly energized and alive.

5 *No bits of business extraneous to the plot.* Well-written farces have plenty of opportunities for sight gags and comic business. These should be plot-driven and found in rehearsal by actors, designers and directors. Don't impose "funny" ideas from outside the world of the play. A gratuitous rubber chicken or contemporary reference can disrupt a play's energy.

6 *Clarify where ground zero is.* Audiences need someone on stage to notice how "wild" things are getting. If outrageous things happen on stage and nobody notices, the audience is robbed of the journey. Someone needs to see how outrageous things are and remind the audience of the absurdity of the moment, even if it is just a butler with a look or a protagonist complaining about his problems.

7 *Every action has an equal and opposite reaction.* If someone insults you, be shocked accordingly. Learn to distinguish between the sparks, firecrackers, gunshots, grenades, bombs, and nuclear weapons that are the artillery of a farce. Vary your reactions. The job of reacting is as important as that of delivering a bomb. I call it "being the crater." Without an appropriate crater, there is no bomb. If someone reacts the same way to every event, audiences will tune them out because they know the actor is on automatic and not reacting in real time to what is going on.

8 *Float the balloon.* Skilled actors set up moments for others to puncture, i.e. just before the arrival of bad news, a guest, a brainstorm, etc. This is part of the fun of a farce—steering the audience's expectations in one direction so that the surprise of the unexpected is visceral. It is akin to volleyball players tapping the ball up in the air for the next player to slam down. This includes setting up shots for your "opponent" to hit. It requires generous and accurate actors willing to set-up for someone else to take the shot.

9 *Make surprises real.* Every night. Don't delude yourselves if a moment isn't working. Acknowledge it in rehearsal and keep working the variables to find what has real impact. If it feels phony, change tactics. Commit fiercely to the moment *before* the surprise happens. This focuses the energy on expecting a different result, and keeps "surprise" reactions fresh night after night.

10 *Use pauses sparingly.* Pauses register shock throughout a show, but can also slow things down. Usually when there is a fresh moment of physical

surprise, a tiny pause is needed to mark the moment. Actual full stops in a farce happen rarely, at the most three or four times.

11 *Never pause within the dialogue* (unless it is absolutely necessary.) Look at films like *Bringing Up Baby* or *The Palm Beach Story*. They are good examples of brisk pace. Brisk tempo is the norm in farce. The last few decades of film and television drama have given contemporary actors a habit of taking unearned pauses. Indulgent thinking/feeling throws wordplay off. The great writer George Kaufman often directed his own shows by listening to actors, not watching them. When he heard a young actor take a long pause in the middle of a sentence, Kaufman asked him "Why did you pause so long?" Proudly, the actor said that in the script punctuation there were eight dots. Kaufman replied, "Make it three dots."

12 *Use variety and dynamics*, not louder/faster. There is a difference between closing cues, and going faster. Actors should speak clearly and with commitment to each line, but their fellow actors should come in right on cue with the response rather than pausing to think. This is very different from everyone trying to talk quickly. The rollercoaster of a farce allows for slow scenes, love scenes, panic moments, moments of seduction, and moments of surprise, but like bricks in a well-made building, there should be very little air between the bricks. Pay close attention to the shifts in tone within the text, but don't disrupt the flow of play between scenes. Typically, the plot isn't rocket science. It doesn't require a lot of reflection to move it forward or to know what the next move is. And if you take too much time, the audience will get ahead of you instead of the preferred other way around.

13 *Try louder/faster.* If none of the above works, then resort to louder/faster. Once in a while, the actors just need to goose the energy to give it that last extra boost to make a scene come to life. This is when louder/faster is appropriate. Make sure the set design facilitates the flow when doors slam, people run, and collisions occur. Eliminate anything that blocks flight paths or gets in the way of a successful climax. Remove what isn't absolutely essential if it is slowing things down, or move it to the side.

14 *Use the full keyboard.* One of the great joys of farce is that it is theatrical. It invites use of the full stage. Use areas that are often neglected. It may only happen in one or two key scenes, but try an upstage corner, behind the couch, on top of the table, under the footstool, or running across the proscenium. Designers should make sets with room to breathe and space for multiple entrances, possibilities for floor traffic, furniture that allows people to move around it, and reasons on the set to go from one side of the room to the other: a phone in a corner, a chess table, a piano, different places to sit, an upstage entrance, multiple doors, and so on. Costumes need to adjust if clothing is too restrictive (unless that is the character's actual dilemma in the plot).

Dramatic structure

To successfully stage a farce, read the play several times and note the major shifts in tone or rhythm. Then develop a score for the show by naming each unit as a reminder of its purpose in the comic structure: the calm before the storm, the big dilemma, the love scene, a new wrinkle, the explosion, the sad aftermath, a bit of hope, the resolution, and so on. Play each scene for keeps within that world order, and play to win. This will give the show variety, surprise, and texture. Too often people assume that because it is a farce or a comedy, everything is played for laughs. No. Sad scenes should be genuinely sad. Quiet moments will contrast loud ones. Shakespeare often inserted a simple, truthful moment in the middle of his most raucous comedies for that very reason. In farce, good storytelling needs to be taken seriously. The protagonist is often not very noble or likeable, which means the audience typically has more fun seeing them get what they deserve. But that needs to be established as well. The moral "compass" of the show needs to be clearly defined and pointed towards true north from the very start of the show, so that the audience knows who to root for and why. If a character is overcome with jealousy, hunger, envy, lust, greed, or revenge, a good actor can tap their own weakness in that area, identify with the motives, and create the right expectations for the audience.

Another challenge with farce is the need for cross-cultural translation. What works in Great Britain may not work as well in America, and vice versa. England has a tradition of butlers and maids, manor houses, and lords and ladies; America's class system is based more on wealthy industrialists, old money inheritance, slavery, and immigrant workers. Comedy relies on recognition, and farcical characters from one culture may not translate well to others. A French farce may have cultural or linguistic references that are not understood in another country. What is considered harmless in one culture may be offensive to others. Conversely, a farcical performer like Jerry Lewis can be more admired in France than he is in his own country. If an American company stages Noël Coward, or a British company stages Kaufman and Hart, they need to find equivalencies that their audiences will understand. England produced *Monty Python* at the same time America produced *Rowan and Martin's Laugh-In*, a good indication that although we speak more or less the same language, our "national tastes" in humor differ.

Noises Off begins with the running gag of an actress playing a housekeeper who forgets her lines and actions while trying to eat sardines in a country manor house interrupted by phone calls and visitors (Escalating Interruptions is a common theme in farce.) It relies on the British audience's familiarity with drawing room comedies and the typical stock character actors who toured the provinces, turning those expectations on their head by making it into a backstage farce. When *Noises Off* is performed in the States, there is an added hurdle to solve. American audiences are less familiar with the setting and the stereotypes. The text uses British idioms and dialects. This does not mean change the setting to Long Island, make the accents mid-Western, and re-write all references. The focus needs to be put on what both cultures share: empathy for people being confused, for people fighting to do their job, and for enjoying the collision of people who have reached the end of their rope.

The same is true when an American farce like *You Can't Take It With You* is played in England. It is set in 1930's New York with topical references that few in England will understand. Should it be moved to London and updated for British audiences? I don't think so. Cultural differences just need to be bridged when staging a farce from another culture. If material is copyrighted, you really can't change the text. So focus on translating the value system by recognizing what both cultures share: a love of family, an acceptance of eccentricity, and a desire to outwit tax authorities. Use action, wardrobe, and clever framing or substitutions to clarify the plot. When doing *The Imaginary Invalid* by Moliere, satirize the doctors and health care systems your audience is familiar with. Once audiences connect the play to their own culture, they can empathize with another value system and enjoy the farce as much as the original playwright intended.

Small scene work

Here are some examples of small scenes that set-up the later explosive scenes. In *Arsenic and Old Lace*, the first few pages establish several synchronized rhythms—the kindness and generosity of the two sisters, the blustery vigor of Teddy, the household's healthy relationship with the local minister and police department, inside jokes ribbing the theater profession, foreshadowing of the love story—all normal scene-setting, meant to be played in a fairly realistic way to establish the world of the play. The only out-of-the-ordinary moment is Teddy yelling charge, pulling an imaginary sword, and running upstairs. But the stage direction "The others pay no attention to this" tells us this is normal behavior in the house. So it is wise to play it straight and let the audience laugh at the fact that normal people in this world are accepting of insane behavior, rather than have the cops and minister over-react at this point in the play to get a laugh, or force the sisters to give away the plot too early by having them act in a crazy, eccentric, or villainous manner. It is important for the actors to invest in their characters and convince the audience this is a kind and generous family, adored by the cops. This exposition plants plenty of seeds of intrigue for the future with hints of experiments in the basement, a missing brother, and the legacy of insanity in the family. Let the words do it, and keep the acting values real as you create a charming and eccentric household.

The first physical game for the sisters happens when they are left alone. Martha notices the tea set out, which means Abby has murdered someone. The comedy comes in recognizing their value system. They are as excited as two teenagers who've made a surprise birthday cake for a best friend. Because Abby made the cake by herself, both she and Martha are extra proud. The focus points at play in finding "the cake" are the tea set, the basement door, each other, and the window seat. Ideally, these points are spread around the set. In rehearsal, the actresses can move to each point physically as they reference it in the lines, or use their eyes to spot it. The energy the sister's share while keeping a secret is what drives the scene. Fully investing in the body language of barely-contained excitement would not be too much here—clasp hands together, jump for joy in unison, or scurry like children on Christmas morning to find a hidden present. Use every millimeter of body language to draw the audience into sharing this excitement. Farce comes to life when actors physically manifest what is at stake.

Once Martha suspects the location, team playing matters. How close does Martha get to the window seat before someone knocks at the door? The actor knocking needs to know the exact right millisecond to interrupt. The actress playing Abby must decide: is it better to lift the lid and drop it? Be just about to touch the lid? Use the left hand or right hand? Lift on an inhale or a held breath? Reach the window and not touch anything? The actors must play this moment together. These are the details that make a funny moment *really* funny. And this is one moment of hundreds in any farce. A great director like George Abbott would just tell the actors exactly how to play it. If there is no comic genius in the room, most actors and directors test actions through trial and error until the best choice is found (usually the one that feels right, flows best, or makes others in the room react.) But the focus is on solving the problem, not trying to be funny. The action of the play needs to move forward. The comedy comes from the audience knowing they haven't hidden a cake: it's a dead body, and nice ladies aren't supposed to murder people and be excited. Manifest physically every thought process so the journey of the characters is visible to all. Everyone on stage has a responsibility to stay physically engaged regardless of who is speaking. Dialogue gives clues to the action, but actors listening must also decide how they will fill the canvas. Always.

The next scene is a love scene that establishes the two normal people in the house—Mortimer and his next-door girlfriend, the Minister's daughter Elaine. It is a proposal scene, and there is a great deal of flirty fun to be had with the status games on the sofa and the physical build-up to the proposal and celebration afterwards. Most importantly, this scene should be believable. We want to like Mortimer and Elaine, and believe their love will survive all obstacles ahead. The text could easily be misinterpreted as a light, breezy scene with 1930's style banter played as if they are already married, tossing dialogue back and forth with nothing at stake. This kills the actual joy for the audience of seeing real people change and be changed. There is no actual line saying "Will you marry me?" so they need to find that moment. If the proposal is played for real and earned in front of the audience, then Mortimer has more to lose. Mortimer needs to keep his aunts' murderous habits a secret from Elaine, lest she dump him as a lunatic as well. This bond to the protagonist then becomes the main pleasure in the show for the audience, who know that through Mortimer they will always know where ground zero is—who is really nuts and who is sane. Watching poor sane

Mortimer heroically deal with a slew of improbable events and end up with the girl while saving his aunts' honor is the engine to the adventures ahead.

The actor playing Mortimer has tremendous opportunities for invention. One big moment comes right after the love scene. It starts as a trio with his aunts. First comes sharing the good news of his engagement to Elaine. All three celebrate in a rush of positive energy that sets up the surprise twist ahead. It is a trio escalation of joy and celebration. The more authentic the joy, the easier it will be to react to the horror coming. Mortimer, changing topics, converts the excitement into a search for a missing manuscript. The aunts, still celebrating, exit for the kitchen to get drinks and cake. Mortimer now has a solo moment that can be milked to the maximum. Preoccupied with finding the manuscript, he hunts around the room in a great mood until he finds a dead body in the window seat. This moment of discovery is huge; it's a big emotional shift from celebrating with his aunts, and a field day for reactions. If you are playing Mortimer, go over the top first, and then choose what fits your production's style best. This is where big is okay.

I directed this show once with a wonderful comic actor from New York (Mike Anthony) who found a full minute of play in this surprise before uttering his next line "Aunt Abby!" George Abbott believed that comedy was like a train that unexpected events derail. At those moments of derailing, he believed there needed to be a minute pause or "take." Some actors squeeze in a famous "double take" at surprises (Bert Lahr), or even a triple take (Edward Everett Horton). Mike combined doing a take with a "delayed reaction," which is great fun here because the audience knows he just saw a dead body and they are waiting for his reaction. Mike stretched the moment for all it was worth, walking several feet away from the window before acknowledging that he had seen something. Sometimes he went back to double check, sat on the box, checked again, lurched around the room to recover his emotional balance and put his eyes back in his head. After rehearsal, Mike would always ask "Too much?" knowing that we both knew how far he milked the moment. But I never got tired of seeing him do it, and it always seemed true to Mortimer's state. Farce gives you the freedom at certain times to physically go all the way. As long as the actor makes the beat register as real shock followed by a thinking person's attempt to deal with the problem, it will work.

In the next scene, Mortimer breaks the bad news to his aunts that Teddy has killed someone, and receives a new shock. The sisters calmly point out that Teddy isn't the murderer, they are. Here, the shock should play differently. Mortimer now fears for everyone's grasp of reality, while the sister's treat this moment like a simple misunderstanding any child would get over. Mortimer's rapidly changing perception of his family fuels a different physical reaction from the previous scene, as this is a different kind of shock. This surprise calls for a more internal reaction, since the problem isn't in the room with a hidden dead body: it is now in Mortimer's own body, as he struggles to reconcile his love for his Aunts with the new fear that they are murderers who have no moral problem

FIGURE 5.2 *Arsenic and Old Lace* (Mike Anthony), The Theater at Monmouth, 2008. Photographer: Ron Simons

with killing. This also sets up a comedy of contrasts between his shock and his aunts' imperturbability.

A skilled actor can vary reactions so that they have somewhere to go in later scenes in a play. The size of the crater (the reaction) should be proportional to the bomb (the surprise). The quality of reaction should express physically the actor's train of thought. How does it make him feel? Like throwing up? Try it. What can he do next? Hide the evidence? Wake the dead man up? Start down that path. Use the low end of the energy scale, where there is more freedom and variety to change tactics, before getting tied up in high-end panic and actions typical of finale scenes. Higher energy limits your options as vocal and muscular tension takes over. Save that for the biggest disasters, which playwrights typically save for the ends of acts. I will address climax scenes later. Remember this is only act I, and you need somewhere to go in act II and III when the evil brother and his sidekick show up, cops arrive, people are tied up, lives are at stake, and entrances and exits accelerate through every window and door. So go big, then get it back under control quickly and soldier on to the next problem.

French theater teacher Jacques Lecoq suggests that when the unexpected happens, the longer it takes you to notice is an indication of your intelligence. If you swing an axe and the head flies off, a normal person notices right away. The clown typically takes longer to notice, continuing forward with the action until they are forced to notice the problem. And like George Abbot, Lecoq believes you pause at the moment of awareness. A dead body requires a reaction, but first pause at the discovery. This clarifies the actor's thought process and tells the audience something's up. After the pause, react, and do what you must to re-establish equilibrium. This sets up the next surprise. In each case, there should be a minute pause marking each moment of surprise. Pauses clarify physical business, just as surely as punctuation makes language on the page more legible. Farces typically cascade from one surprise to the next, with moments of restored equilibrium and a new status quo in-between.

Pauses can also come from people watching an action rather than the doer. Buster Keaton's deadpan pause is often a reaction to other people or objects in motion, not his own actions. Watch the Marx Brothers on film do one of their routines. When Harpo pulls out scissors and cuts off people's ties, the other brothers typically watch him move from one absurd choice to the next. Pauses are registered by Groucho and Chico, who punctuate Harpo's continuous stream of actions with their own reactions and commentary. I bet if you slow the film down, you can also see Harpo take minute pauses. His movements are relaxed and "easy" to watch, not frantic. His actions are clear and deliberate.

Another small scene full of surprises is in act I of Feydeau's *A Little Hotel On The Side*, with the Pinglets and their old friend Mathieu. This is a sub-plot that returns at the climax of the show. The sarcastic banter between Mr. and Mrs. Pinglet is disrupted by the jarring speech pattern of their friend Mathieu, who is a stutterer (only when it rains.) This is a language game, pure and simple. How close can Mathieu come to saying something inappropriate, rude, or insulting as the Pinglets draw him out? How physical does the stutter get? Is there a gesture Mathieu repeats? It is a classic escalation scene, as actors use vocal color and polite restraint, mild aggravation, and complete outrage to react to Mathieu. If you reach a peak, try understatement and see what happens. Deadpan is a good gear to shift to when Mathieu announces his last surprise—that he has arrived for a month, with several children and their luggage in tow. The stutter scene is seven pages long, so don't let the audience become as frustrated as the Pinglets. Vary the pitch, speed, and dynamics from deadpan to apoplexy (not necessarily in that order) and stay focused on moving the story forward.

In the finale of *A Little Hotel,* the stutter returns at just the right/wrong moment as Mathieu is about to reveal what he knows and incriminate his friends. A thunderclap is heard (pause) and a downpour makes his stutter return, preventing the police from being able to sort out what happened. Pinglet and company are saved from ruin. Frustration at the stutter earlier becomes delight when it returns in the end to save the day. The stutter scene at the end involves more people than the first small scene, but because they have such bearing on each other, try rehearsing the scenes back-to-back to find the right balance between them. Then put them in the right order.

Climaxes

The climactic door-slamming scenes with multiple actors and plot threads coming together are the biggest challenges in farce. Let's look in detail at three examples: Feydeau's *A Little Hotel On The Side*, Kesserling's *Arsenic and Old Lace*, and Kaufman and Hart's *You Can't Take It With You*. At the Actors Theater of Louisville 1993 Cultures in Context Conference on the George Kaufman–Marx Brothers collaborations, the showcase production was a revival of the musical *Cocoanuts* directed by Jon Jory. The highlight of the show was a routine finely-tuned by the Marx Brothers, in which two hotel rooms sit side by side facing the audience with a door between them, entrance doors upstage, with beds and trunks to hide under. As one person exits, another enters with no one seeing the other person. With split second timing, the fun of these near-misses was beautifully staged. When I asked Mr. Jory how they did it, he said they spent forty hours of rehearsal on that one scene alone. The investment was worth it. (Side note: getting doors to swing and slam well on a set is no easy task: it may require some carpentry adjustments as you rehearse.)

Focus

When you have a big scene with numerous people and multiple events on stage, the audience's eye needs to be told where to focus. An easy way to think of it is to imagine the scene having an invisible "basketball"—a spot the audience focuses on. This spot can move around the room so that the audience sees specific moments and hears specific lines of dialogue, including sudden shifts from one side of the stage to the other. If you do have two things happening simultaneously, try to place them upstage and downstage of each other in the same visual frame so that audiences can see both without glancing left and right. The "toss" in focus can come from an actor pointing, shouting, or moving in the direction of the next moment. A sudden outburst, exclamation, entrance, or abrupt change in height or energy can also take focus. People on stage should notice and react to where the focus is to help guide the audience's eye. If everyone is moving, stillness will take focus. Every bit of business must be orchestrated in big scenes, even if it plays for just a half a second. If too much is going on for the audience to take in, cut back a bit on the activity. Do less first, layer in more as needed. Once you find the balance you will reach that sweet spot described by the character Frederick in the film *Children of Paradise* where the actor's and audience's heart beats as one.

Once everyone knows a traffic pattern in a complex scene, run it slowly as a group to clarify where to be, when to move, and on which line. Then pick up the pace. Do it in ten-second chunks. Play red light/green light with the action, so that the director can make adjustments. Start layering in advanced moves, like someone hopping over someone crawling by, or someone picking up a lamp and swinging it just as someone else ducks. You can also break the scene into five or six key moments and treat it like a slide show. Create a stage picture at each key moment and connect the dots by moving from one stage picture to the next.

Every farce has at least one group scene where things get out of hand. In *Blithe Spirit* it is the séance scene. In *A Little Hotel on the Side*, it is the police raid on the hotel. I devote time early in rehearsal to these scenes and return to them frequently so that by the time the show opens they all flow smoothly. Once a scene is rough-staged, use any spare time to add finishing touches: a sharper gesture at the end, a small grace note in the middle, some physical comedy with an object along the way. As with any fight scene, have a combat call to mark through the busiest traffic patterns before every performance. It helps guarantee actor safety and serves as a good warm-up each night.

Another method, especially in a scene with a lot of sound and dialogue, is for the stage manager or director to use a whistle that freezes the action as soon as the blocking is off or someone is lost. Go back to the beginning and start again. Continue starting from the top and running until you can run cleanly through the whole scene safely without stopping. Try it in slow motion with no dialogue, repeat with dialogue at half speed, and then again at normal tempo. If there are breakable objects at risk of falling on the set, remove them or take them out of the line of fire before the action begins.

Working the big scenes

The comic mayhem at the end of act II in Kaufman and Hart's *You Can't Take It With You* is the result of multiple plot points coming together, a collision that literally explodes in a shower of fireworks. Only three pages long, it involves every character in the cast (except for one introduced late in act III) and requires choreographed movement patterns as complex as a well-run razzle-dazzle play in basketball.

The set-up for the climax is the "dinner party turned disaster." The wealthy Kirby couple comes to the eccentric Vanderhof household on the wrong night, and sees enough to convince them their son is marrying into the wrong family. A parlor word game threatens the Kirby's relationship. Alice breaks up with Tony, and the love story derails. This very low note in the play needs to register to contrast the acceleration of the climax to follow. Kaufman gives a clue to the dynamics on stage by asking that the entering FBI agent's first line, "Stay right where you are, everybody," is *spoken very quietly*.

Using the idea of titles, I would call the first beat of the finale "the sex game," then "the break-up," "the feds interrogate," and "the explosion." In the first beat, the players gathered around the room with pencils and pads are writing down answers to a word association game Penny has started. The fun of this scene is in the accelerating feud between Mr. and Mrs. Kirby as their tempers rise, contrasting the helplessness Alice feels trying to stop the game or change its direction. For blocking, the focus is on the Kirbys. Most people are fairly stationary, but there may be some movement by the Kirbys out of their seats as the argument gets more heated and Alice tries to intervene. This scene (which is about four pages long) accelerates rapidly, so start as simply as possible, as if nothing could go wrong. Everyone in the room is a choral "mirror" to the fight, registering with various degrees of shock or delight what is being said by the Kirbys. This choral response amplifies the disaster building up between the Kirbys. The fight gives Mrs. Kirby a strong reason to call the dinner off and leave early, so her embarrassment is key. This starts the exit towards the main door, and the unexpected break-up of Alice and Tony.

The "break-up" beat is short, about half a page, but it is a real change in tone: a shock to Tony and a moment of despair for Alice's family. The focus shifts to Alice and Tony, and the sexual dysfunction of the Kirbys fades from view. Since the Kirbys are heading for the door, this is a good place for Alice to take focus and go against the exiting tide. Alice can move far downstage or cross the stage away from the door, so that a big gulf is created spatially between her and the Kirbys. Everything is now unresolved and destabilized, with an awkward goodbye from the Kirbys covering everyone's hurt feelings. This is a perfect low point in a farce to go from Bad to Worse. A federal agent walks into the spatial void center stage with a quietly threatening command and now has instant focus from everyone around him. The sadder and messier the emotional stew at the end of the break-up, the better the joy ride in the wild last three pages when the feds arrive.

"The feds" begin the real finale, and the focus of the scene shifts to them. They enter quietly and begin to interrogate people. They take control of the room and immediately complicate innocent statements with suspicions of nefarious plots. In the middle of the scene, a pipe left burning in the basement ignites fireworks that explode throughout the final page of dialogue, as everyone runs for cover. To choreograph this scene, I used a technique I found when staging a production of John Guare's *The House of Blue Leaves,* a tragi-comic farce with a similarly explosive act ending. In that play, a live bomb is literally tossed from character to character, including three nuns, before it explodes. The action is complicated by everyone making a mad dash for two free tickets to see the Pope on his visit to New York City. I rehearsed each actor's flight path one at a time through the whole scene, starting with the person who enters with the bomb and the first person to grab for the Pope tickets. I then started adding characters in pairs and trios as needed, making adjustments as more people were on stage. This method also worked well for *You Can't Take It With You.* With eighteen people in the scene, I rehearsed each actor's movement and dialogue alone, with the stage manager saying the missing people's lines, until everyone knew their actions individually. I then ran it with three people, then six, and so on until everyone could run the scene together on stage in real time.

The first time I staged the explosion scene, we had the good fortune of being able to hire pyro-technicians to light real fireworks with actual gunpowder. The technicians needed very clear places in the action to ignite bombs, showers of sparks, flying rockets, and other special effects. This forced us to plan carefully ahead of time and do all the blocking before adding the actual explosion effects. We mapped out a "score" for the explosions, and ran it first with the stage manager calling out the effects vocally for the actors, i.e. "boom!", "Rocket flies by!" and "shower of sparks at the door!" One of the best dynamic moves we made was to put in a pause right after Penny yells "My manuscripts! My manuscripts!" This let everyone believe it was over, and they all exhaled. This "breather" was just a set-up. A second later, the biggest explosions of all went off and a giant rocket blasted across the stage. The first time we ran it with real fireworks it was so spectacular we all burst into applause. It was *so* exciting and overwhelming! The scene got a standing ovation every night. You can be sure everybody came back from intermission to see how it would all wrap up in act III.

In *A Little Hotel on the Side,* a police inspector shows up near the end of the play for the denouement, restoring order through a completely improbable sequence of events. But this is not the most difficult scene. The hotel bust at the end of act II is the busiest in the play. The action starts close to a boil from earlier shenanigans; ghosts, people in disguise, and best friends are all within a door slam of each other in a shady hotel loaded with rooms, stairs and hallways. The audience is primed for everyone colliding. The spark to the explosion is the police raid. But the dynamic is quite different from the bust in *You Can't Take It With You.* In that play, the scene starts low and quietly builds toward the fireworks. In *A Little Hotel,* the pace accelerates *before* the cops enter, and bursts immediately into a full-scale chase scene á *la* Keystone Kops. The dynamic is one of close calls and misses as people try to avoid each other. It is a "contact" scene, with lifting, pushing, pulling, grabbing, and running. Map out the action on a white board using colored pens to draw floor patterns for each pair, group or solo actor, like a complex football play with O's for patrons and X's for cops. Make the misses as close as possible. Use durable clothing in rehearsal that won't tear so you can add costume grabs, holds, and lifts. Choreograph slowly and deliberately, then speed up gradually.

And don't go too fast. Look at a classic "chaos" scene in a Marx Brothers movie. It's amazing how relaxed everyone is in the "Don't make a sound" sequence in *Duck Soup.* Like a well-oiled machine (which came from years of doing the act on stage), the mayhem is much slower than you might imagine. Pauses and counter-intuitive movements build suspense and ensure actors' safety. When cues are close together, they are very close, but no one is panicky. The timing at the start of the door routine (one person exits as another tries to enter) is impeccable. This scene is a variation on the hotel scene I mentioned earlier in *Cocoanuts,* only this time everyone is disguised as Groucho. The final payoff in the scene is the mirror routine. Groucho sees Harpo through an opening in the wall and Harpo pretends to be his reflection. Groucho plays with his image in the mirror, a surreal and magical scene that is a complete rhythmic shift from the previous chase, an interlude of divine comic genius. Look for such change-ups in any farce finale. The energy should be focused and managed. A staged fight is choreographed to control the energy and create the illusion of violence; a big farce scene is orchestrated to create the illusion of pandemonium, when in fact everyone knows exactly where to go.

The "traffic patterns" in a finale aren't just physical: they are also emotional. The climax in *Arsenic and Old Lace* is the last twelve pages of the play. It starts

FIGURE 5.3 *Arsenic and Old Lace* (Mark Cartier, Mike Anthony, Bill Van Horn), The Theater at Monmouth, 2008. Photographer: Ron Simons

when police arrive at the Brewster house searching for a missing cop-turned-playwright who has besieged Mortimer all night with pitching his new play. When the head cop makes a phone call to police headquarters to "call off the big manhunt … We got him," meaning the missing cop/playwright, crazy brother Jonathan overhears and thinks he has been caught.

Rapidly, all the plot threads collide: Teddy goes to Happy Dale Asylum, Jonathan gets arrested, the cops find their missing colleague, Mortimer joins Elaine, and the aunts get in one last murder. Physically the focus follows the action in the dialogue as indicated in the script, and does not call for complex choreography. But embedded in the resolution are several key surprises that need to register: the cops never take the bodies buried in the basement seriously; no one believes the aunts when they say they are murderers; Jonathan tells the truth for once and no one believes him; everyone is thrilled to have the bad guys caught and the truth buried except Jonathan, who realizes he has been outfoxed; and Einstein signs the aunts' commitment papers and escapes in plain sight as the cops are discussing what he looks like. The action moves quickly enough to sweep the real truth under the rug, but if each cast member reacts individually and collectively to these moments as they happen, registering these surprises emotionally gives audiences a much more pleasurable catharsis than just barreling through the scene. Sharing with the audience the truth of what is really going on by carefully placing pauses in the action or "passing the basketball" of focus to make the climax legible and engaging is critical to understanding the story.

FIGURE 5.4 *Arsenic and Old Lace* (Ian Austin, Bill Van Horn, JP Guimont, Matt Archimbault), The Theater at Monmouth, 2008. Photographer: Ron Simons

Another technique I find useful for large group scenes is to use up-tempo music appropriate to the world of the play. The bouncy jazz music of Raymond Scott (which was used in so many Warner Brothers cartoons), opera overtures, or the finale of Beethoven's Fifth or Ninth Symphony come in very handy. These are pieces of music with multiple themes and syncopated rhythms. Once a scene is blocked and running smoothly, try playing music underneath it, not in performance but as a rehearsal technique. Use it on an entrance or exit to goose the actor. It helps fuel their physical energy and prompts actors to project their voices. It gives everyone a larger sense of the feel of the scene. It helps actors understand that their job in the play is like that of the bass, the triangle, the trumpet, or the drums, and that no one person has to try to be the whole orchestra. You can also skip recordings and just sing a whole scene as if it were an operetta, or use a live drummer to add accents to a run-through.

For *Arsenic and Old Lace* I played tracks from Don Byron's *Bug Music* at the first rehearsal and told everyone that that was the energy I wanted to aim for in the show. In *You Can't Take It With You*, I used big band music of Duke Ellington, Count Basie, and Benny Goodman to lead into and out of each act. For Feydeau, I used accordion music and French film soundtracks to accent the action, and kept some of it in the show for underscoring. Using music in rehearsals helps actors play briskly and maintain momentum. As music gets faster, clarity is even more important. It takes skilled musicians to hit every

FIGURE 5.5 *Arsenic and Old Lace* (David Greenham, Dan Olmstead, Bill Van Horn, Ian Austin, JP Guimont), The Theater at Monmouth, 2008. Photographer: Ron Simons

sixteenth note crisply, and the same is true for actors in a farce. And if you can afford it, live music is always the best.

To me, the job of acting in a farce is like the job of a musician playing the finale to Beethoven's Ninth Symphony. Know your part within the whole. Stay on tempo with your fellow actors. Make each note clear. Play only your notes. And play it passionately and accurately. Physicalizing farce requires a kind of musicality in the actors that is as important to the life of the play as knowing your character's motives or understanding the play's dramatic structure. Real fights are chaotic, messy, and brief. Farce climaxes are carefully planned and exquisitely layered to prolong the audience's pleasure.

References

Plays

Feydeau, Georges and Maurice Desvallieres. 1984. *A Little Hotel On The Side*. Translated by John Mortimer. London: Samuel French.

Frayn, Michael. 1982. *Noises Off*. London: Samuel French.

Guare, John. 1966. *The House of Blue Leaves*. London: Samuel French.

Hart, Moss and George Kaufman. 1937. *You Can't Take It With You*. New York: Dramatists Play Service.

Kesserling, Joseph. 1941. *Arsenic and Old Lace*. New York: Dramatists Play Service.

Additional reading

Baker, Stuart E. 1981. *Georges Feydeau and the Aesthetics of Farce*. Ann Arbor, MI: UMI Press.

Lecoq, Jacques. 1987. *Le theatre du geste*. Paris: Bordas.

Lecoq, Jacques, 2006. *Theater of Movement and Gesture*. Edited by David Bradby. Abingdon: Routledge.

Mason, Jeffrey. 1988. *Wisecracks: the Farces of George S. Kaufman*. Ann Arbor, MI: UMI Press.

Spolin, Viola. 1963. *Improvisation for the Theater*. Chicago, IL: Northwestern University Press.

6

COMIC GESTURE USING "VIEWPOINTS"

Christopher Olsen

"Viewpoints is an open process, not a rigid technique," say the authors of *The Viewpoints Book* in their introduction (Bogart and Landau 2005). This process leads to an exploration of movement and bodily "compositions" and quickly expands into creative approaches a director takes when working on a production with a group of actors. Anne Bogart and Tina Landau, both stage directors, drew from their vast experience working with dancers and actors when Bogart started the SITI Company with Tadashi Suzuki in 1992 focusing on the development of collectively created theatre productions. What was vital to the rehearsal process was an extensive exploration of "viewpoints"—a creative philosophy which they turned into techniques for developing an ensemble of performers through the application of movement. These creative journeys were divided into categories called "viewpoints" which were applied through the examination of time, space, and composition. Adherence to viewpoints emphasized rigorous physical preparation and ensemble building that encouraged performers to develop coordination and sensitivity via observing and integrating with each other.

The viewpoints introduced in the book were the following: tempo, duration, time, repetition, spatial relationships, topography, shape, gesture, and architecture. For example, a series of exercises exploring the viewpoint of "shape" might evolve in the following manner: A group of performers make a circle and one person moves into the center of the circle and creates a shape out of his/her body. Then 2–3 members of the circle join the original person and construct a new shape based on the three of them. Finally, all the rest of the members of the group join in and a shape of multiple bodies is created from the individual expressions. Then the reverse process occurs and several people leave the constructed shape and return to the periphery. Finally, everyone has gone back to the circle except for the original person who created the initial shape. The group then tries to recreate the entire process from start to finish.

These exercises can be expanded to include voice and language and they can eventually become a basis for the blocking of a scene. In this chapter I plan to focus on only one of the viewpoints—gesture—to explain how this viewpoint can contribute to the development of comic acting.

The study of gesture has historically been the focus of linguists and anthropologists in their examinations of culture. Linguists often regard gesture as a form of language and approach the analysis of cultural norms and social practices via a verbal/non-verbal axis. The famous French anthropologist, Marcel Mauss, researching how the body functions in different societies described the most elementary dimensions of physical behavior as varying widely such as the way people stand, sit, walk, use their hands, and eat and sleep (Bremmer 1992: 15). One of the first known rhetoricians was Quintilian in the first century AD, who in describing his fellow Roman citizens created an opposition between "rhetorical" and "theatrical" gestures. In looking at the way people gave public speeches, he was able to distinguish between gestures from the speakers that were derived from inner emotions from those that were intellectually thought out (Graf 1992: 38). By the Medieval era, gestures were considered a passageway "from nature to culture"—what was considered natural and instinctive became incorporated into a cultural sign system that defined daily life and relationships. For example, people were instructed to respect the personal space of social superiors by bowing and keeping a distance from them or to show humility in a religious setting by genuflecting in front of an alter or kissing a cleric's hand. Eventually by the seventeenth and eighteenth centuries gestures became more associated with cultural manners and the rules of etiquette including expressing signs of friendship, peace offerings, insults, agreements, social introductions and farewells, and eating habits. By the nineteenth century, children from the "upper classes" were expected to be taught manners and gestures that revealed their "civilized" superiority whereas gestures that offended "polite society" were regarded as unwelcome and relegated to the behaviors of the lower classes. Some modern theorists have analyzed specific gestures of speakers to underline their logical progression of arguments. They have divided gestures into four categories:

- ideographs which are gestures that underline a particular verbal part of an argument;
- pointers, which emphasize specific statements;
- pictorial gestures, which are represented in mime for what is being discussed; and
- batons, which are gestures that accompany the rhythm of what is being said.
  (Dromgoole 2007: 59)

Even in the twenty-first century, there are numerous books published about how to interpret and express gestures to help one "translate" the signs from other cultures with catchy titles such as *The Do's and Taboos of Body Language around the World* (Axtell 1991) and *Multicultural Manners: Essential Rules of Etiquette in the 21st Century* (Dresser 2005).

Obviously, the idea of gesture has pervaded comedy ever since performers started identifying their characters by a set of gestures. Ancient Greek and Roman comedy—and later *commedia dell'arte*—created a variety of characters that were defined by gestures from the squatting, squirming servant to the conniving, threatening master who does not hesitate to hit his underlings at any time he feels undermined (hence, the emergence of the word "slapstick"). The gestures marking differences between characters from different social ranks as well as between genders (ancient Greek men would be expected to walk more quickly and confidently whereas women would be expected to take smaller, more "feminine" steps) would become the basis for many comic encounters.

So what is gesture and how is it defined in comedy? Since the ancient Greeks, theatre practitioners, philosophers, and social critics have written about stage comedy and how it is formulated. Aristotle wrote about gestures as one of the comic elements in satyr-plays where performers adopt a "ludicrous" comic mask (Cooper 1922: 176). Brecht wrote about gesture as an outward expression for an actor's inner emotions and how a single gesture can become a metaphor for the emotion of the entire character (Brecht 1964: 139). Probably the critic who addressed the idea of gesture in comedy in greatest detail was Henri Bergson, who wrote three essays under the title "Laughter," which provided a theoretical framework for the production and reception of comedy (Bergson [1900] 1956). In the section on "the comedy of character," he points out that the attitudes, gestures and movements of the human body can generate comedy because they remind the audience of a machine. We laugh, Bergson writes, because a person doing comedy can turn himself into a series of mechanical gestures that give the audience the impression that the character is a thing rather than a human being. Bergson draws a distinction between gestures and actions by stating that actions occur when the entire body is engaged whereas gestures are expressed in isolated parts of the body. Gestures comprise the attitudes, the movements, and even the language from a character to express itself for no more reason than a "kind of inner itching." In other words, gestures are involuntary and automatic whereas actions are intentional and conscious. He ends by writing that there is something "explosive" about gesture and that when audiences become fixated with the gestures of the characters rather than actions on stage, we are in the realm of comedy.

Jacques Lecoq, the famous movement and acting teacher, often wrote about gesture and how actors can create the fundamental elements of their performance through the observation of real life. He divided gestures into three categories— that of action, expression, and demonstration. He notes that gestures of action emerge from the body alone whereas expressive gestures include emotions and basic psychological states. Gestures of demonstration are punctuated with spoken language which often replaces them (Lecoq 2006: 9). Lecoq has been very influential in redefining the rehearsal process—in particular, for theatre groups who are collectively creating new "text" using movement, language, and transformative techniques. The concept of "transformation" has been used as a creative exercise by many prominent theatre groups including Joseph Chaikin and The Open Theatre in the 1960s. This rehearsal exercise—called "Transformation"—requires actors to divide the stage into four quadrants and begin a scene in any one of them based on the following premise: each quadrant represents a unique "world" demanding a different physical approach from the performers—for example, one quadrant might be characterized by abstract concepts such as freedom or claustrophobia; the second, asking for a scene to begin in a different historical period; the third, featuring a world of non-human creatures; and the fourth, a realistic depiction of everyday life. Actors would begin a scene in one quadrant and when one or more of them decided to move to another quadrant all the members would have to follow suit and "transform" themselves into the new world. This would continue for an entire workshop and test the ability of actors to work in multiple settings and to maintain creative connections among themselves.

Bogart and Landau divide gesture into *expressive* and *behavioral*. Expressive gestures are more abstract in composition. They are created by finding something behind the movement such as a feeling or idea. Behavioral gestures are more familiar in everyday life and represent recognizable signs made out of everyday communications. They often start from clichés but can eventually be modified to bring out a "greater consciousness." The movement from expressive to behavioral is like moving from the abstract to the concrete. The gesture may be formed from any part of the body—from the feet to the head—and the process can develop from there. The purpose is for performers to widen and deepen their arsenal of gestures by exploring them more comprehensively. Instead of just coming up with a predictable gesture expressing only one thought, the process of going from abstract to concrete exploration can produce not only a more original gesture but one that can be expressed from a variety of perspectives. Each gesture should have a beginning, middle, and end. Table 6.1 presents some examples of expressive and corresponding behavioral gestures.

TABLE 6.1 Expressive gestures and behavioral gestures

Emotion/attitude	Expressive gesture	Behavioral gesture
Frustration	Moving feet up and down	Crossing arms and swaying
Sadness	Curling up in a small space	Putting hands together in a prayer position
Embarrassment	Rolling on ground like a ball	Looking down with hands clasped
Claustrophobia	Rotating body and making it fit	Laying on the floor and in to increasingly smaller spaces, shrinking
Sweetness	Moving in small curves; opening	Bowing slightly, smiling body with hands facing out

Below is a series of activities which serve as suggestions for running a workshop exploring gesture. The workshop is divided into three parts and operates as separate stepping blocks towards the greater understanding of gesture. After students become familiar with these three areas, then the class can move towards applying gestures to comic bits and eventually to scenes and entire stage plays. The final part of the workshop functions as a separate rehearsal which might be utilized (incorporating some of the gesture exercises) as a precursor to the blocking of a specific scene from a play.

Working with gestures—begin with clichés

One of the oldest rehearsal ploys by stage directors is to run a scene with the actors having their arms tied behind their backs. They are forced to express their emotions and intentions via the rest of their body instead of waving their arms all the time. Pointing with the index figure has become such a cliché that actors are often asked to eliminate that gesture and find other gestures for expressing the same feeling. By actors not relying on their arms and hands to express their feelings, the exercise opens up opportunities for them to explore other areas of their bodies.

In the first series of exercises, everyone forms a circle and one person creates a clichéd gesture such as wagging the index finger as if one was disciplining a child. Everyone repeats that gesture and it is repeated by the original person several times while the group members respond in like. Then the clichéd gesture is replaced by a gesture conveying the same idea but with a greater consciousness. Everyone individually tries to come up with a different kind of gesture which derives from the same idea as the original. The teacher (or director) can ask for gestures emerging from different parts of the body. For example, instead of the hands, the gesture begins in the back, or in the feet, or another area of the body. As the original clichéd gestures are "returned" by individual members to the group, new ideas begin to emerge for expressing that thought and those ideas become more nuanced and creative.

This cliché exercise can continue for some time and gives the group a sense of collective creativity but at the same time rewards individual contributions. Other clichéd gestures to explore might include the following:

- putting your hands together in prayer;
- applauding by clapping your hands;
- putting your hand up to signal for someone to stop;
- waving goodbye;
- blowing a kiss;
- showing the middle finger;
- thrusting your arm up in approval (such as people do at sports events);
- winking your eye;
- rotating your hips in a suggestively sexual way; and
- shaking your fist in a threatening manner.

The point of this exercise is to become aware of one's own stage choices for a character which too often are created by using clichéd gestures rather than taking the time to explore more creative choices using other parts of the body.

Experimenting with different gesture groups

Now the group explores different types of gestures and concentrates on the following categories:

- mimetic
- medical
- mechanical
- iconic
- idiosyncratic
- culturally specific
- soliciting
- receiving
- contradictory and
- transformative.

Other categories can be included but the teacher/director should be aware of the time limit and choose as many as he/she can administer without having the students feel rushed or overwhelmed. Begin with the basic area of mimetic gesture. This is essentially copying each other as children so often do with their friends.

Mimetic

One student walks across the floor as if they were totally unaware that anyone was around. The walker should be moving automatically and spontaneously without trying to embellish any movement. The idea is that the person is walking as close to his/her "natural" gait as possible. After a few times, the other students individually try to walk across the floor trying to imitate their classmate as accurately as possible. Balance, rhythm, and posture are important characteristics to observe. When everyone has done the walk, the students try to recall the movements of one or two of their classmates and they perform the walk while the others try to guess the classmate being imitated. This exercise helps students observe others as they walk in public and to observe specific gestures within a basically mundane and ritualistic activity.

Medical

In gestures dealing with bodily functions (or malfunctions), it is important to observe how the rest of the body compensates for the malfunction. If one is limping, the entire body has to maintain a balance that often tries to minimize the rocking motion of the person moving. Each student chooses a gesture that suggests a medical issue in the body such as having a stomach ache, dealing with a mosquito bite, or having to go to the bathroom. The purpose of this exploration is to find gestures that reveal this medical problem and to experiment with how the entire body reacts to an isolated medical issue. Other areas to explore include sneezing or coughing incessantly, experiencing very cold or warm conditions, feeling nauseous, and having a sore throat. Many gestures created derive from that single malady in the body and each student should be given a chance to explore a number of them.

Mechanical

Referring back to Bergson's concept of mechanical gestures, this is an exercise where students try to identify and incorporate daily activities that are repeated in an almost automated manner. The way you put your clothes on, how you greet strangers, typing on a computer, and preparing food might be activities that you perform mechanically on a regular basis. Each student locates a mechanical activity that he/she performs daily and recreates it. At first it is re-enacted slowly and deliberately and later the students can adjust the tempo, duration, and intensity of it. The idea is that the activity produces a series of gestures that the student can recreate and then manipulate. Through this exercise, students should be able to identify a number of mechanical activities that they perform daily and reproduce them regularly.

Iconic

These are gestures that seem to have a universal meaning and arouse a similar reaction in many people. The most obvious examples would be gestures that generate a strong emotional reaction and those that demand a reaction from a crowd or group of people. One can think of gestures like the Nazi salute or a moment of crowd jubilation when a goal is scored in a soccer game. These gestures require a group response rather than just an individual one so the exercise takes the form of a group of students coming up with an iconic gesture and displaying it in unison. Divide the class into several groups of students and each group comes up with a gesture that they all can share in.

Idiosyncratic

These gestures are created as specific to an individual and derive from a deep-rooted examination of a character. Here is when the exploration into expressive gestures can pay dividends because you as the performer are coming up with a unique set of gestures pertaining to a character. You need to explore the history and motivations of the character you are playing and experiment with gestures that turn into an extension of the inner life of the character. How often does one gesture become the principle identifier of a stage character especially in comedy!

Culturally specific

This category is often a lot of fun because it allows students to imagine themselves as very different human beings who move and gesticulate in a variety of ways. For example, when one travels abroad, one realizes how words from the same language can have totally different meanings. For example, the Englishman may say "Do you know where I can pick up a pack of fags?" as he alights from the airport bus in Manhattan, and is told that he is very rude but that there are plenty of gay bars in New York he can go to. He is totally taken a back saying his wife is trying to get him to kick the habit but it is hard. "Fags," of course, mean cigarettes in Britain. Gestures, too, have a variety of meanings in different cultures such as who and how to kiss strangers, telling people off with insulting fingers, and eating with your hands. Many a traveler has got him/herself into trouble by not researching some of the local customs and gestures of the country they are visiting. The "culture" can be very real and understated but can also be an exaggerated rendition of a mythical fantasy. In this exercise, the class picks a culture such as Ancient Greece, modern Italy, or the Wild West in America. This is a collective exercise where the class comes up with a series of gestures related to the culture being explored. In our examples, gestures related to Ancient Greece can be in the form of exaggerated gestures, frequent enunciations to the heavens (where presumably greater interaction with the Gods occurs), and manly acts of fighting. Also, since the body is more exposed (literally) and celebrated, the emphasis on physical interaction between and among the sexes might be explored. In the case of modern Italy, the students would explore modern behavior in Italy such as speaking and expressing oneself more vigorously with one's arms, making flirtatious sounds and gestures between sexes, and generally touching each other with greater abandon than in countries like the USA. Gestures from the Wild West might include a slight drawl in one's speech, walking with a wider stance as if you had been on horses all your life, and wearing/adjusting a hat. After the students have finished their gesture exploration, they recreate it as if it was an improvised scene but using just gestures and sounds. They are exploring the semiotic idea of what the "culture" is comprised of and which is something they can draw from while rehearsing a play from a similar culture.

The final four categories below deal with how gestures are generated and are divided into the following.

Soliciting and receiving

A soliciting gesture refers to a gesture that begins with your movement and attempts to illicit a response from another character. The obvious example is a greeting which requires a corresponding gesture in turn. A receiving gesture allows a character to initiate a movement and then asks the recipient to provide a corresponding one. For example, a receiving gesture to a gesture of greeting would be to return the same gesture but perhaps more fervently. Break the group into couples and have each student experiment with soliciting/receiving gestures. Play both ends of the communication and play with a variety of gestures. Manipulate and explore the gestures using variations of tempo, intensity, and focus. By the end of the exercise, the student couples should be able to produce a variety of encounters using gestures and their variations. It is another excellent exercise for ensemble building.

Contradicting

A contradictory gesture is a gesture that is normally not associated with your "normal" behavior. It is often a gesture that is surprising or off-putting—or was not expected—and contradicts the movements associated with your character. An obvious example of this is when men adopt "feminine" gestures or vice versa. An exercise I often use to warm up a class is to create an improvisation where a bunch of male friends are standing/sitting around and deciding what to do that evening. I begin by using a few men from the class for this exercise. I then do the same for a group of girlfriends and then I switch them around. The guys become the girls and have to use some of the gestures that the women used and vice versa. Initially, the performers make everyone laugh by exaggerating and distorting the gestures but as the exercise develops both groups begin to experiment with more specific and concise movements that are assumed to be appropriate for one or the other gender. For example, guys tend to greet each other more boisterously than do girls, whereas girls tend to touch each other more often while conversing than do guys. With contradictory gestures, ask students to work alone first and develop gestures and "their contradictions." Start by asking them to create gestures for their character type such as an old man or a little girl. Experiment with simple gestures that seem to represent the character. For example, you have an older person gesturing like a younger one and vice versa or a weightier person moving like a thinner one. Another series of gestures might include a character which usually functions with a lot of poise and commands respect from his/her associates using vulgar and degenerate gestures which culminates in a different behavior. On the other side of the coin, you have a simple and clueless character turning into a refined and erudite person. The idea here is you are progressing from one set of gestures associated with the character to another which is associated with the opposite. "Opposites attract" is indeed a hallmark of comedy playing.

Transforming

Finally, the transformation exercise allows the class to function as a group where a gesture from one member can open the door for the entire group to join in the transformation. As mentioned earliet, the transformation exercise revolves around "conditions" for four acting spaces (quadrants) on the stage. Each quadrant turns into a new world bringing with it a new set of gestures associated with it. When one character starts a new gesture in a quadrant, the other members of the class find themselves moving into that world and integrating their gestures to become a part. This exercise tests a performer's ability to not only be able to adapt to a new world of gestures but to observe classmates creating them and learning how to integrate into their world. A greeting of a 2014 "fist-touch" between good friends transforms into a Renaissance bow and kissing of someone's hand in a sign of deference.

Gesture and creating comedy: exercises

Now we are ready to use gesture in our exploration of acting comedy. For the purposes of this chapter, I will primarily use Bergson's comic terms although there are others that can be equally applied. I want to begin by using his terminology so that one can see how quickly the creation of gestures can develop into simple, comic moments and then, by extension, transform into extended comic scenes. Let us start working with three basic concepts:

- repetition
- exaggeration and
- inversion.

In exploring repetition, each performer explores an individual gesture (with a beginning, middle, and end) and continues to master it by repeating it. For example, one might wave goodbye or raise one's hands to indicate someone should stop approaching them. Once that gesture is mastered then one begins to experiment with the size, intensity, and speed of the gesture. Alternate and experiment with different tensions associated with the gesture. Finally, decide on a level the gesture might take and move from the behavioral to the expressive area and back and see how that gesture can be adjusted to make a clearer, more original expression. Then, integrate the gesture into a short scene with another performer. He or she will have done the same preparation as you have done but using a different gesture so the "confrontation" between the two of you will feature two different entities with their unique gestures. By repeating each gesture during the improvised scene the performers can find ways of integrating comedy into the repetition of the gesture at specific times. For example, the performer waving goodbye becomes increasingly frustrated because the other character won't leave; or one character tells the other not to approach by raising their hands and then discovers that that person wants to seduce him/her. As you can see a repetitive gesture can inform the comic scene and set up a conic interchange which is repeated in a variety of ways that changes the course of the comic narrative. The scene is simply based on a couple of gestures that are "expanded."

In working with exaggeration, one can pursue the same line of exploration by creating a gesture and exaggerating it. For example, take a gesture like jumping up and down and exaggerate it. Explore different ways of jumping up and down such as turning your body slightly or gesticulating vigorously with your arms or legs. Then try to express a basic emotion like anger and start finding a way to jump up and down to facilitate that emotion. As a result of this exploration, your physical gesture may lead you to create an older person, let's say, who happens to be ranting about something or it may lead you to become a child, who is throwing a temper tantrum. In both cases you are exaggerating the simple gesture of jumping up and down and merging it with a basic behavior pattern from some kind of character. Remember, anger does not just stay on one level but can build and recede as the scene develops. Your partner will also be working on a different exaggerated gesture—let's say, rocking back and forth while whimpering. Both gestures then are integrated into a basic scene between the two characters, each of you utilizing your "exaggerated" series of gestures and confronting each other. When the initial exercise is over both performers then integrate their exaggerated gestures into the scene and add improvised dialogue and see if they can sustain the narrative for a couple of minutes. When the exercise is over, the teacher and student performers discuss how the exaggerated gesture became a part of an improvised character. How often do we see a couple of *commedia dell'arte* characters "counter-balance" each other using the repeated, exaggerated gestures mentioned above like when an angry master admonishes his mistake-prone servant. By the use of exaggeration, each gesture can contribute to developing the relationship between two comic characters and heighten the confrontation within a scene.

Inversion is particularly challenging because it involves exchanging one gesture for another—often total opposites. I previously mentioned the exercise I have used in class when guys try to act like girls and vice versa using what they feel are typically gender-based gestures. Inversion means you adopt/exchange the gestures of your partner and vice versa. Suddenly the frightened, quivering servant becomes the aggressive, arrogant master and vice versa. The idea here is to associate a gesture with its opposite and to create two characters who can complement each other. One thinks about the famous comic partners, such as Laurel and Hardy or Abbott and Costello, and one realizes that the contrasting gestures associated with each comic contributed greatly to their joint humor. Laurel would often do his signature gesture of taking off his hat and screwing up his face and scratching his head while Hardy would sit down with a look of disgust and tell Laurel, "That's another mess you have gotten us into."

In this exercise two performers experiment with contrasting gestures and then exchange them. Characters which seem awkward doing an activity and try to overcome that obstacle often use gestures that are repetitive, exaggerated, and more mechanical. When a man is walking in high heels, his awkwardness and his attempts to move smoothly and alluringly produces comic moments. When characters put on disguises and pretend to be another person, it is often not only the disguise that is comic but the character's exaggerated and repetitive gestures to "be convincing" as that character that gets the laughs. Many bedroom farces use moments of disguise when characters "disappear" into another character and mimic them. Their increasing desperation to hold on to their disguise is what creates much of the comedy. The British farce *Charley's Aunt* by Brandon Thomas, for example, makes full use of a series of gestures for the main character who must continually disguise himself as his elderly aunt. What makes the technique of inversion so comic is that characters are forced to adopt unfamiliar gestures (for them) and to integrate them into a "new" character; the humor arises from their struggle to master that transformation, often desperately.

Speaking of transformation, the idea of transforming oneself in comedy relates to putting yourself in the middle of two realities. Transporting a gesture from one level of reality into another can be another great source of comedy because an audience sees the performer take the step between two parallel narratives. For example, one often sees characters begin to laugh at something and then something dawns on them that make them realize an alternate situation and the laughing turns into crying. The act of transforming the pace, tempo, and intensity of the change—can lead to a wonderful comic moment. You can see this done when someone starts to flirt with someone else in conversation and then they begin to grow more familiar with each other and before you know it they are dancing a wild tango as if they had suddenly fallen madly in love. Another example could be a scene of a duel between two characters which are preparing themselves meticulously for an encounter to the death—except it is with kitchen utensils and concerns who can make the most elaborate cake. Transporting one set of gestures associated with a scene from one reality to another produces comedy because the audience is allowed to see the change a character makes by shedding one reality with a given set of gestures and transporting those gestures to another reality.

I want to end this chapter by giving you some examples of scenes from established comedies where gesture exercises could be used in rehearsal. Obviously, purely improvisational work always requires performers to incorporate gestures in the development of a created text. As I mentioned above, any kind of collective creation also lends itself to applying some of these exercises during the rehearsal process. Tackling established comic plays, however, sometimes intimidate the novice, comic actor and he/she becomes so concerned with the language of the character that the accompanying bodily expression sometimes takes a back seat to the verbal humor. One has to work on both simultaneously and find both the inner and outer life of the character using voice *and* movement. Both should work in tandem and become a joint process. Here is a part of a scene from Moliere's *The Imaginary Invalid*. The hypochondriac, Argan, is constantly bullying his sly servant, Toinette, usually threatening her with bodily harm and then collapsing in exhaustion after his outbursts:

Argan:	… Where are you, you invalid-killer? Toinette! Minx, bitch, whore!
Toinette:	I'm here.
Argan:	Why, you evil—
Toinette:	Look what you did, you and your impatience. You yelled so loud I whacked my head running into a door.
Argan:	You treacherous little—
Toinette:	Yes, it's all your fault. See the bump? It stings. It stings so bad!
Argan:	Over an hour ago—
Toinette:	Ow, ow, ow—it's worse.
Argan:	You abandoned me—
Tonette:	My head is dead.
Argan:	Shut up, so I can bawl you out properly.

(Bermel 1997: 16–17)

You can see by this short piece of dialogue that the relationship between master and servant is very physical—and, of course, quite abusive. One of the first exercises I would try with the two characters is to create a series of basic gestures for each and use them in a kind of fencing match with each other. Toinette seems to be always distracted and therefore runs into furniture and doors whereas Argan seems always ready to chew her out by demanding that she come to him. Argan might, for example, create a gesture that continually wants to grab Toinette like he would do to his dog but she always finds a way of eluding his grasp. You can see how the language of the characters can be bolstered by a creative choice of gestures to enhance the characters' movement.

In a more modern example, Christopher Durang's *Beyond Therapy* is a comedy about a bisexual man, Bruce, who in the first scene is on a blind date with a socially, repressed woman, Prudence. The characters almost seem to have a cartoonish quality about them but it would be a mistake to over-exaggerate the characters and go for broad comedy. The following exchange between the two characters at a table at a New York restaurant illustrates some of the humor:

Bruce:	In some ways you're a little girl. And in some ways you're a woman.
Prudence:	How am I like a woman?
Bruce:	You … dress like a woman. You wear eye shadow like a woman.
Prudence:	You're like a man. You're tall, you have to shave. I feel you could protect me.
Bruce:	I'm deeply emotional, I like to cry.
Prudence:	Oh I wouldn't like that.
Bruce:	But I like to cry.
Prudence:	I don't think men should cry unless something falls on them.
Bruce:	That's a kind of sexism. Men have been programmed not to show feeling.
Prudence:	Don't talk to me about sexism. You're the one who talked about my breasts the minute I sat down.

Bruce:	I feel I'm going to cry now.
Prudence:	Why do you want to cry?
Bruce:	I feel you don't like me enough. I think you're making eyes at the waiter.
(he cries)	
Prudence:	Please, don't cry, please.
Bruce:	*(Stops crying after a bit)* I feel better after that. You have a lovely mouth.

(Durang 1983: 9–10)

You can see that one of the principle gestures for the character of Bruce is his crying but the gesture must have a beginning, middle, and end because often he is about to cry and then stops himself. The actor playing Bruce has to find that unique gesture for "about to start crying" because the audience identifies the character with that tendency. Prudence, on the other hand, has to find a gesture that she keeps returning to when she is uncomfortable in a social situation. She is constantly trying to break out of her shell but when confronted often retreats back into it. The retreat requires a gesture that is repeated.

I would like to introduce one final example from David Ives's "Sure Thing," one of the scenes from his play *All in the Timing*. Ives has a gift for satirizing banal dialogue and he often puts characters together who seem so contrived and disingenuous because their language is filled with simplistic banter which are often outright lies. Ives uses a wonderful comic technique of "rewinding" pieces of dialogue so that the characters must stop and start their dialogue again as an off-stage bell rings. The actors must recover instantly and "redo" their lines except for a few word changes and in addition produce a slightly different gesture for each line. Ives is, in part, making fun of people who are always "scripting" their forthcoming dialogues ahead of time in order to gain an advantage. Bill and Betty have just met in a café and he has made a move and sat down at her table:

Bill:	You weren't waiting for somebody when I came in, were you?
Betty:	Actually I was.
Bill:	Oh, boyfriend?
Betty:	Sort of.
Bill:	What's a sort-of boyfriend?
Betty:	My husband.
Bill:	Ah-ha. *(bell rings)* You weren't waiting for somebody when I came in, were you?
Betty:	Actually I was.
Bill:	Oh, boyfriend?
Betty:	Sort of.
Bill:	What's a sort-of boyfriend?
Betty:	We were meeting here to break up.
Bill:	Mm-hm … *(bell rings)* What's a sort-of boyfriend?

Betty:	My lover. Here she comes right now! *(bell rings)*
Bill:	You weren't waiting for somebody when I came in, were you?
Betty:	No, just reading.
Bill:	Sort of a sad occupation for a Friday night, isn't it? Reading here, all by yourself?
Betty:	Do you think so?
Bill:	Well, sure. I mean, what's a good-looking woman like you doing out alone on a Friday night?
Betty:	Trying to keep away from lines like that.

(Ives 1995: 10–11)

Again, you can see how the sudden switches of temperament using the same verbal line can create the comedy. It is the recovery of the character at one given moment that gives him/her another chance to "redo" the exchange. Each time Bill says, "What's a sort-of boyfriend?" the actor must accompany the line with a subtle gesture change. The humor lies in both these characters persistently sizing each other up by telling lies about themselves and observing how the other reacts. What is so important is achieving the split-second timing that the scene requires from both actors so that the gestures and responses are quick and organic as the bell continually interrupts and signals for the next moment of exchange.

I hope I have offered you some insight into the exploration of gesture and how the smallest of gestures can open up a world of comic moments. If you think about the great comic actors of stage and screen, so often their work was defined by signature gestures associated with characters they created. Charlie Chaplin's sauntering walk (created by his wearing his oversized left shoe on his right foot and vice versa) or his customary way he doffed his hat while greeting attractive women are testaments to his dedication to developing very detailed gestures. He was known for being a perfectionist and would work on minute routines for days until he got it right. I believe that great comic acting is a gift but it is also a craft that all actors can develop and utilize. Even some of the great plays that are often seen as somber and serious contain many moments of comedy because of explorations into gesture. I can't, for example, imagine how Samuel Beckett's *Waiting for Godot* can be presented successfully without bringing out the physical comedy between the two erasable main characters.

References

Axtell, Roger E. 1991. *Gestures: The Do's and Taboos of Body Language Around the World.* New York: John Wiley & Sons.

Bergson, Henri. [1900] 1956. "Laughter." In Wylie Sypher (ed.), *Comedy*, 59–190. Baltimore, MD: Johns Hopkins University Press.

Bermel, Albert (ed.). 1997. *A Dozen French Farces: Medieval to Modern*. New York: Limelight Editions.

Bogart, Anne and Tina Landau. 2005. *The Viewpoints Book: A Practical Guide to Viewpoints and Composition*. New York: Theatre Communications Group.

Brecht, Bertolt. 1964. "Short Description of a New Technique of Acting." In John Willett (ed.), *Brecht on Theatre: The Development of an Aesthetic*, 136–47. New York: Hill & Wang.

Bremmer, Jan and Herman Roodenburg (eds.). 1992. *A Cultural History of Gesture*. Ithaca, NY: Cornell University Press.

Cooper, Lane. 1922. *An Aristotelian Theory of Comedy, With an Adaptation of the Poetics and a Translation of the Tractatus Colslinianus*. New York: Harcourt Brace & Company.

Dresser, Norine. 2005. *Multicultural Manners: Essential Rules of Etiquette for the 21st Century*. Hoboken, NJ: John Wiley & Sons.

Dromgoole, Nicholas. 2007. *Performance Style and Gesture in Western Theatre*. London: Oberon Books.

Durang, Christopher. 1983. *Beyond Therapy*. New York: Samuel French.

Graf, Fritz. 1992. "Gestures and Conventions: The Gestures of Roman Actors and Orators." In Jan Bremmer and Herman Roodenburg (eds.), *A Cultural History of Gesture*, 36–58. Ithaca, NY: Cornell University Press.

Ives, David. 1995. *All in the Timing*. New York: Vintage Books.

Lecoq, Jacques. 2006. *Theatre of Movement and Gesture*. Ed. David Bradby. London: Routledge.

Thomas, Brandon. 1993. *Charley's Aunt*. London: Samuel French.

7

PLAYING WITH LANGUAGE

Wit and wordplay

Merry Conway

> Nothing is more foolish than to talk of frivolous things seriously, but nothing is wittier than to make frivolities serve serious ends.
>
> (Erasmus, *In Praise of Folly*, 1511)

> Wit is the unexpected copulation of ideas.
>
> (Ben Johnson, *Rambler*, 1752)

Using language in a playful and dexterous way is one of the pleasures of human communication. Juggling words, playing with meanings, and wriggling through innuendo quicken the pulse and mental functions. There is an experience of *levity*, a lightness of mind and body. On the stage of a theatre, wit and wordplay brings disparate meanings and ideas together, stimulating an audience to perceive new connections about the characters and themes of the play.

These days we might tend to think of wit as decorative repartee, but its etymological roots reach down to an earlier entwining with wisdom. By the Renaissance, *esprit*, the French word for wit, meant "good sense that sparkles," implying light and movement; it also meant "spirit," suggesting an essence. To John Locke, in the mid-seventeenth century, "wit lies most in the assemblage of ideas and [puts] those together with quickness and variety" (Hill 1993). The mastery of complex comic language is an essential tool for actors.

I began working with language skills in order to support actors performing Shakespeare. George Stuart Gordon has described the thrill with language that overcame speakers of Elizabethan English, with "its power of hospitality, its passion for free experiment, its willingness to use every form of verbal wealth, to try anything." This shared excitement produced the "fertility and happy-go-luckiness … the linguistic vitality of its greatest master" (Gordon 1928).

Contemporary productions often try to sidestep Shakespeare's linguistic richness. A common strategy is to cut as many witty exchanges as possible, which prevents the audience from engaging with the complexity explored in these passages—and hacks away at the play's meaning as expressed through language. Or a director might ask actors to speak very quickly, leaving the audience behind and feeling slow or stupid, as though they have missed the jokes. Another approach is to act out every piece of wordplay physically, like an extended game of charades, adding a "mime track" to the text, which slows down the performance and is tiring for both actors and audience. Still another strategy is to ignore the wit altogether—to have the actors speak the witty lines in the same tone as the non-witty ones, and replace the wit with stagecraft or some other form of comedy to bridge the gaps in communication.

To reawaken the *pleasure of language* in the actors and ultimately in their audience, I have developed a pedagogy for approaching complex texts. The goal is to create an atmosphere of joy and excitement in which the allure of wordplay sweeps us into the shimmering world of the author. In the following pages I describe a sequence of exercises with which I launch this process. Although I began this work with the texts of Shakespeare, I have applied it successfully with students to a variety of comic material, including Molière, writers of the Restoration, Oscar Wilde, Gilbert and Sullivan, Lewis Carroll, Edward Lear, Noel Coward, The Marx Brothers, Mae West, Joyce, Beckett, Ionesco, The Goon Show, Peter Cook, Monty Python, Steven Sondheim, Tom Stoppard, and Steven Colbert. Comic writers and devisers who are creating their own language-conscious work have also found these exercises helpful.

Rekindling the child's love of language games

I start with play and joy because *playing* with language is a basic human activity. "In the long game of evolution … humans' extended period of imaginative play, along with the traits it develops, has helped select for the big brain and rich neural networks that characterize *Homo sapiens*" (Dobbs 2013). It is pleasurable to create, to hear and to speak wit and wordplay, as we awaken the mind and the spirit. An energetic pleasure vibrates from the text and must be experienced each time by the actor, who must in turn ignite it in the audience.

From a developmental perspective, the babbling infant, repeating syllables in various sequences—*do-do-da, da-do-da*—is learning to put sounds together but also the transitions between syllables, a critical stage in the acquisition of language. Humans share this learning process with song birds, whose chicks also babble, putting the syllables of their song together as they learn it from their parents. After the babbling stage, human children gravitate to phonological structure. Playing with sound for sound's sake is a happy pastime.

Did you ever, iver, over
In your leaf, life, loaf,

See the deeval, divel, dovel
Kiss his weef, wife, woaf?
No, I never, niver, nover,
In my leaf, life, loaf,
Saw the deeval, divel, dovel,
Kiss his weef, wife, woaf.

(Sanches and Kirshenblatt-Gimblett 1976)

Although the meaning of words becomes more important to wordplay at a later age, we all retain an appreciation and pleasure in the sounds of words, through alliteration, onomatopoeia, and rhyming of all kinds. If you have any doubt that this pleasure lasts into adulthood, watch the "vessel with the pestle" scene from the 1956 movie *The Court Jester* with Danny Kaye (see www.youtube. com/watch?v=PotoHuLEJRY). For five delightful minutes of comic confusion and linguistic acrobatics, Kaye, as the frightened knight, tries to remember the instructions of the helpful witch, who tells him about a cup filled with poison he should avoid in the upcoming fight: "Listen carefully. The pellet with the poison's in the vessel with the pestle. The chalice from the palace has the brew that is true." For a kick, repeat these lines three times rapidly out loud—with a sense of urgency!

"The young are lovers of laughter and therefore adept at wit," wrote Aristotle in his *Rhetoric*. When I teach wit and wordplay, I start by reminding students of their own childhood pleasure in using language. Some immediately recall knock-knock jokes. Others have difficulty recapturing the period when language was limitless and not weighed down by the duty of communicating sensible thoughts. Awakening and reclaiming our linguistic heritage is an essential component of building the skills of wit and wordplay in adulthood. The knock-knock joke introduces puns—at the thrilling moment when children realize that words can have more than one meaning. Riddles are usually puns in the form of a question. Clapping games are very physical and provide rhythm and the fun of play. Nursery rhymes introduce rhyme, narrative, and morality in a condensed form.

I ask students to bring in early texts that demonstrate wordplay: tongue twisters, knock-knock jokes, riddles, nursery rhymes, and songs we recite together, often with accompanying hand gestures. We learn clapping games in pairs. As gestures speed up, the excitement in the room is palpable. In subsequent classes I use these childhood games as warm-ups. I do this to connect with the pleasure, to get the tongue and the mind working more elastically. We walk around the room saying words that begin with specific sounds, such as *zzz, shhh, kkk*, as a way to re-awaken our sensitivity to sounds.

In the following pages I describe a set of circle explorations that I have conducted with undergraduate and graduate students, professional actors and writers. Each game adds a wordplay skill. I intersperse these games with scene-writing assignments, done in pairs, using skills we've practiced. We also read aloud passages from plays and other forms of literature and analyze the use of wordplay. We weave between both ends of the wordplay structure, from the building of condensed wisdom (such as proverbs) to the pulling apart of common sense (such as puns).

I have invented many games to fill a need. Others I have adapted from the rich legacy of improvisational games I learned in the 1970s, or from games commonly played in childhood. Following the descriptions of the exercises are examples from classes I have taught. I am grateful to my students for helping me to refine these games and for the pleasure of creation we feel as we play them.

Everything I do involves bringing the body into the work. We begin with thirty minutes of physical exercises, to get the juices flowing. This warm-up includes playful physical and vocal exercises and is designed to bring humor into the room, so that the whole acting instrument is ready to participate. Without the committed energy of the body, the fire for wordplay, and the pleasure, soon dies. We remain standing and moving through most of the class, so that the work never gets "heady."

"Make a large circle ..."

This is how we begin many exercises. The circle locates us in a familiar physical setting for a game, uniting us in a communal activity. A fundamental element of wordplay is that action-driven linearity is not the goal, but rather enjoyment of play. The shape of the circle reaffirms the pointlessness. As Susan Stewart writes in her book *Nonsense*, "Circularity is implicit in the reversibility and repetition of play. When 'means' are the object rather than 'ends,' when one's goal is precisely to never arrive anywhere, the circle emerges as the form of this activity" (Stewart 1978). So we make a circle. Any time the energy needs to be shaken up, students can run out to the corners of the room and come back, re-forming the circle in a different configuration.

In the games I play with students, the focus is not on winning but on listening and being spurred to invention by others. I foster an atmosphere of commitment to the group and support of one another. I have found that people risk more and compete less if they feel supported and can focus on developing specific skills. The experience of group cohesion also helps to establish the atmosphere I look for in performance: actors *sharing* the wit with the audience, rather than showing how clever they are as individuals.

One-word story

The group, standing in the circle, makes up a story, sentence after sentence, with each person contributing just one word. Release your word as fast as you can, overriding the "clever student" internal monitor that would like to evaluate choices and select a word for its inventiveness and intelligence. There are only two rules in this game: say your word immediately, and accept whatever word you are given as the "perfect" word. Of course it is not the word *you* would have chosen! That's the whole point. You could easily write your own story with all your own words.

The one-word-story game is about opening our mental sphincters, as I like to put it, so we can outsmart the inhibitions to spontaneous speech. There is an internal monitor censoring everything we say. As soon as we learn *how* to speak, we are taught what not to say. Internalizing these rules is imperative for success in society. "If you can't say anything nice, don't say anything at all." "Don't speak unless you're spoken to." These phrases teach us to be appropriate and correct in our social intercourse—and also impair our access to spontaneous creative wit and wordplay. One of the joys of reading *Alice's Adventures in Wonderland* and *Through the Looking-Glass* is that Alice exemplifies social inhibitions, and is overwhelmed by the topsy-turvy world of incorrect, untethered, and socially unedited creatures.

In our wit and wordplay room, there is great delight as all sorts of mad stories come into being, full of twists and turns. Inappropriate, scatological images appear out of nowhere. The goal is to act as a conduit, passing energy from one person to the next. Listen to the images and characters coming to life. Although you cannot make sense of it all, trust that the group will make sense. The one-word-story game fosters the understanding of the communal activity of making sense. It's important to find content that engages you, or you will lose interest.

> Pants are good on men and women, especially when it's sunny. Easter time is family-oriented with friends and family. Arriving blessedly late, we decided to talk about converting our faith, together to pray. Hatless, dressless, clothesless, we frolicked and leapt and dived into the flowers. Nuns, priests, laymen, lame men, walked away from the festivities. They dragged their cassocks, with habits, slowly down habitual paths.

Several variations build on this structure later in the progression. Once people are getting the hang of it, you can make one-word sentence stories with each word beginning with a sequential letter of the alphabet. Any hope of managing to make sense word by word is challenged by the metalinguistic requirement to follow the alphabet. Brain cells awaken audibly.

> Agnes bet cautiously during engineering flight going home. I, Jane, kept longing morosely, numbly, of pining questioning rather stubbornly, terrifically, until vacation was x-ed yesterday. Zebras, able, etc.

Our minister's cat

Next is an old "car game" we used to play on those endless road trips, before electronic devices kept children entertained. This is a game of alliteration, except that I never use that word, or any of the proper terms, until the end of our time together. Then I present a list of the technical terms, along with the game in which we used it, so the students can associate their mastery with a name. Many students have had bad experiences in dreary or oppressive English classes: using the proper names can take them right back there. Instead, we go for the fun of "finding words all beginning with the same letter" to describe a cat.

Choose a letter, such as O, and start by saying "Our minister's cat is"—and a word that starts with O—"orange." Around the circle, everyone says a descriptive word beginning with the letter O. The rule is that you are not allowed to repeat, so you are encouraged to listen rather than spend time thinking of a word, since there's a good chance someone will say "your" word before you do, and if you're distracted you won't hear.

We begin finding vocabulary we haven't thought of in a long time, or have never used out loud. In the desire to invent something, we start to create sophisticated hybrids or bastardizations, which the circle receives with chortles of delight. I allow wiggle room the first times round. When students are more skilled, they enjoy the rigor of the rules and it doesn't overpower their pleasure. I follow the greater balance of pleasure to exactness. As we get past the more conventional words, we start making up some amusing ones.

> Our minister's cat is orange, octagonal, opinionated, oval-shaped, ordinary, overheated, opulent, onerous, ovarian, overt, obese, ogre-ish, over-the-hillish, ovulating, owlish, Oscar-winning, open, odd, Oedipal, odious, old, Olive-Garden-eating …

Too much attention to playing the game *correctly* can be distracting. Two types of anxiety can creep in. One is that rules are more important than the play. Nonsense! The second is a fear that under-regulated play will lead us to utter chaos. Both affect the group's feeling of possibility and fun, which are the foundations of building skills in wordplay.

Rather than discouraging the anxious student, I give the anxiety a shape to inhabit. The Pedant is a character that personifies the energy of the strict rule-keeper. I always have on hand a small bell and a ruler with a ridiculous and colorful pointy hat. I invite people to express their apprehension in an exaggerated way as the stick-waving Pedant. They can begin to make fun of it, to diffuse its power. We enjoy the performance and return to an atmosphere of adventure.

Synonyms

The next game is about words that share meaning (synonyms). I send out a starting word, for example, "big." Each person in the circle adds a word that means something similar. As we go around the circle numerous times, the variety springing from that initial word is amazing to hear.

Colossal, mansion-sized, gynormous, monumental, obese, universal, grand, Herculean, super-sized, Grand Canyon-like, Value-sized McDonald's, Big &Tall Men's Shop-ish ...

Copiousness

In the age of texting and tweets, people lack confidence in language's capacity to express their thoughts and feelings. They shrug their shoulders and mumble, "Whatever." Starting to read Shakespeare, students have asked me, "Why couldn't he just say it in one line?" or "Why does he have to go on and on?" There are many reasons for the happy outpouring of language in Shakespeare's time, but that is a longer discussion. Fundamentally, the actor needs to know and feel that experience can be expressed through language, that there is a *need* to articulate experience in the common venture of doing theater.

I work to develop a capacity for expansive language by introducing the idea of copiousness, a term that evokes the cornucopia, or horn of plenty, and the Roman goddess Abundantia, with her ample bosom exposed, in Rubens's 1630 painting. The humanist teacher and scholar Erasmus revived ancient Greek and Roman culture for his contemporaries in sixteenth-century Europe. In *De Copia* he describes how words and thoughts could be used to greatest effect: abundance, eloquence, variation—all of it compared, amplified, delighted over. Hugely popular at the time, *De Copia* was probably a text that Shakespeare read as a child, his language still forming (Erasmus 1963). Without sophisticated linguistic skills you couldn't survive at Elizabeth's court, since quickness of speech was equated with nimbleness of mind. The Queen spoke several languages and was celebrated for her quick and spontaneous wit.

To approach copious amplification, we make a circle and return to the first exercise, the one-word story. As the sentences unfold, be aware when the word you choose *describes* something (an adverb or adjective) and emphasize that for the next person in the circle by making a definitive physical gesture. The next two people continue with an additional descriptive word. The series of three can be either alliterative or synonymous. Then the story continues as before. In this refinement of the one-word story, we *amplify* the language, moving the story sideways, out of its forward thrust.

> Robert went willingly, westernly, whimsically over the hill. Sally didn't like anything Robert did. When Robert was feeling funny, hilarious, fine, he loved to run ravenously, robustly, righteously, onto the train.

Now we are ready to look at an example Erasmus himself used: "Your letter delighted me very much." In the circle we repeat the sentence but vary it by increments, at first changing only one word, for example, "letter" with "epistle." Then we change how sense is communicated, using metaphor, synecdoche, etc., adding images and rhetorical flourish to fill in the scene.

Princes have never had the type of wealth your letter brought to me, kings have never reigned over the country as you reign over my heart, and God himself must have come down to spread you with divine inspiration, for you to have written such a beautiful letter to my lowly, humble soul.

This is a pleasurable way to experience *variation*, and gives students confidence in their ability to amplify. We develop a more subtle understanding of variation, how much is too much and what is good taste, when the excitement of abundance is in the air. To inspire his students, Erasmus lists 130 of his own variations.

Antonyms

Now it's time to look at words with opposite meanings (antonyms). Still in the circle, one person turns to the next and says the first in a pair of opposites, such as up/down, night/day. Then we move on to two-word opposites: high sky/low earth. If the class were geared toward Shakespeare, working with antithesis would be the next step. Many of his comic couples battle with words in bantering flirtation, for instance. The exchanges are most successful when the antithesis is acted out physically, as a game: we need to know who made the point, who won and who lost. If one picks up opposing words from his or her partner to play with, the audience has a real enjoyment of this game of love, and can keep score while also seeing into the minds of the characters.

Rhymes

The opening exercises with children's nursery rhymes and clapping and counting games reawaken the pleasure of rhyme. Appreciating rhyme requires that the comic actor *enjoy* and *maximize* the repeated sound, so that the audience may also enjoy it. Students are often embarrassed by rhyme, which decreases their enjoyment. Elaine Stritch, coming to the end of one of Steven Sondheim's great song lines, miraculously arrives at the rhyme with a devilish glint in her eye, and then lets us have it. Her enjoyment of the rhyme allows *us* to enjoy it. The power of the rhyme can certainly be felt in hip-hop performers who combine rhyme with rhythmic line structure to produce great complexity.

To gain skill in making rhyme, start with someone saying a line of doggerel, such as, *I took a short walk down the road*—light verse in unspecified meter. The next person says a line of about the same length, with the last word rhyming. So we produce couplets with rhyme endings AA, BB, CC, DD, etc., around the circle. We aim for sense and continuity of image and narrative. We begin to hear the length of lines and become adept at matching them. In the beginning, you may doubt you can do this, but you can!

> She loved so much bread she thought she'd die,
> So she grabbed a loaf and stuck it in her eye,
> The grains, they stung; the yeast infected,
> Is that a sesame seed I've detected?

Then we make it a bit more complicated, continuing the narrative with the rhyme scheme ABAB CDCD, etc.

> Underneath the bridge of doom,
> There stood an old, old man,
> Who, when he hopped upon his broom,
> Made up a cunning plan.

After looking at limericks we can recall together, I ask students to write their own. The limerick lends itself nicely to satire and wordplay. It has origins in fourteenth-century rhymes and later mad-songs sung by wandering beggars known as Mad Bedlams. Shakespeare's Edgar in *King Lear* uses this type of mad-song in his disguise as Mad Tom (Legman 1964). The invitation to be witty and play with language and reversal of thought makes limerick-making a good exercise. Tom Stoppard uses the limerick form in a scene of *Travesties*. The James Joyce character begins with a straightforward soliloquy in limerick form:

Joyce: Top o' the morning!—James Joyce!
>   I hope you'll allow me to voice
>   My regrets in advance
>   For coming on the off-chance—
>   B'jasus I hadn't much choice!

As the scene unfolds in which Joyce is looking for money, the form is cleverly divided among the characters:

Carr: The Boche put on culture a-plenty
>   For Swiss, what's the word?
Joyce: Cognoscenti.
Carr: It's worth fifty tanks
Joyce: Or twenty-five francs
Carr: Now … British culture …
Joyce: I'll take twenty.

>   (Stoppard 1974)

Proverbs

And now to invite some wisdom into the room! This series of games starts out by grounding us in the familiar, common-sense world—which soon unravels. On the simplest level, proverbs, adages, and other gnomic expressions are condensed pieces of wisdom in a memorable form. Proverbs often use metaphor to help us remember. A bird in the hand is worth two in the bush. In the past, people memorized hundreds of these sayings to help them through life. Financial tip: Neither a borrower nor a lender be. (Polonius to his son Laertes!) Health tip: An apple a day keeps the doctor away. Morale boost: If at first you don't succeed, try, try again. There's a whole book of Proverbs in the Bible. Erasmus compiled hundreds of Latin proverbs for boys to learn. The tradition continued into the twentieth century. In flea markets I have found several pocket-sized, well-thumbed books people must have carried around with them, one hand-written, with proverbs to live by.

Sometimes there is a dead silence as we form our circle and collectively try to remember some proverbs. Where have they gone? Some people insist that they don't know any. Gradually, as we begin to warm up, the unconscious inculcation begins to be exposed. Soon proverbs are flying out. We pronounce each one in a mock-serious tone and touch our fingertips lightly together, imitating a wise person. This keeps us more embodied with the idea of sharing wisdom. We look at how proverbs express a point of view. Its familiarity and pithy form give it the ring of truth.

I once heard the proverb specialist Wolfgang Mieder talk about how US presidents always use proverbs in their speeches so that their message will appear more trustworthy. Proverbs unify. "Ask not what your country can do for you, ask what you can do for your country," JFK said in his inaugural address.

We use the circle to create a pool of proverbs we can draw from—everything from Shakespeare to contemporary advertising—and begin to explore the themes: all the proverbs about fools, or beauty, or the home, or nature. In this way we come to appreciate the full range of these sayings.

After repeating the proverbs in full, we start sending half of one across the circle. The person receiving completes the proverb. The circle loves it when the person responsible for the second half either makes a mistake or is perhaps unfamiliar with the "real" proverb and has to invent something.

The mismatch becomes the start of our next step, which is to undo wisdom with wordplay! We formalize the matching of the first half of a proverb with an "incorrect" second half. Most enjoyable are the hybrid proverbs that make lexical, but not logical, sense. Reading the scene in Lewis Carroll's *Alice's Adventures in Wonderland* with the Duchess and Alice is useful here, as the Duchess extracts a (confounding) moral from whatever Alice says.

> "Tut, tut, child!" said the Duchess. "Everything's got a moral, if only you can find it." And she squeezed herself up closer to Alice's side as she spoke …
>
> "Somebody said," Alice whispered, "that it's done by everybody minding their own business!"

"Ah, well! It means much the same thing," said the Duchess, digging her sharp little chin into Alice's shoulder as she added, "and the moral of *that* is—'Take care of the sense, and the sounds will take care of themselves.'" …

"It's a mineral, I *think*," said Alice.

"Of course it is," said the Duchess, who seemed ready to agree to everything that Alice said; "there's a large mustard-mine near here. And the moral of that is—'The more there is of mine, the less there is of yours.'"

(Carroll 1946)

Another way to undo a proverb is to start with the "real" half—"You can lead a horse to water"—and continue with the second half in prose that is both literal and unmetaphorical, and also the *opposite* of the pithy style of the first half: "but you cannot then bring his mouth to the water source, try to force to open his lips and draw the water into his mouth." This jumble of styles highlights the purity of the original. More from Alice and the Duchess:

"I quite agree with you," said the Duchess; "and the moral of that is—'Be what you would seem to be'—or if you'd like it put more simply—'Never imagine yourself not to be otherwise than what it might appear to others that what you were or might have been was not otherwise than what you had been would have appeared to them to be otherwise.'"

"I think I should understand that better," Alice said very politely, "if I had it written down: but I can't quite follow it as you say it."

"That's nothing to what I could say if I chose," the Duchess replied, in a pleased tone.

In my advanced classes we move on to tweaking proverbial structure in many other ways: jumbling, altering by one word, punning, and adding a non-sequitur or a contrasting sentence. One person sends the first half across the circle to a second person, who messes with it. The second person starts with a new half, and passes it to someone else to complete.

You can't buy—a woman's horse.
Ask not for whom the—hammer falls.
Monkey see—fishes fly.
Those who forget the past—grow old.
An old fool—plays a lot of games.
Life, liberty and—the windows of my mind.
For all we know—life is short.

Punning

> To see this age! A sentence is but a chervil glove to a good wit.
> How quickly the wrong side may be turn'd outward.
>
> (Feste, in Shakespeare, *Twelfth Night*, III: 1)

It is unfortunate that puns occupy a diminished status these days. We often apologize with, "Pardon the pun," or even anticipate a groan—*when we have magically turned the meaning of one word into two!* The pun is a glorious and central part of wit and wordplay. I push students to regain a healthy delight they may have lost with their last knock-knock joke. Appreciation for, and thrill in, puns is essential to do Shakespeare and other complex texts. I'm glad to report that a renewed enthusiasm for the glorious pun is currently being displayed every month at the New York chapter of Punderdome, a large gathering of enthusiasts who compete to win the best pun, as judged by a human clap-o-meter. One of my former students won runner-up in a recent event.

I use the broadest definition of the word pun, because punning always involves a switch, of one for two: either one word with two meanings, or one word with two inferences; or two words for one, each with their own meaning. I start in the circle by asking who can tell me the meaning of "bear." People throw out: *naked ... a furry animal ... unadorned ... to show (as in teeth) ... minimal (as in bare necessities)*. We start to get excited as we realize all the possibilities. After trying the same thing with other words, we move on to making punning sentences, using body parts: *Don't* elbow *your way in ... I* knee-d *you ... you have a* skull-*pted body ...* Quickly students are shrieking with delight at a good pun with geographical words—*Can you* Peru-*se this?*—or vegetables. In these games, you don't have to go in order, you can just call out examples as they occur.

The pun has a rich and long history. Shakespeare knew that plays on words made the audience listen more attentively, in order to figure out just how the words were being used. Puns make meaning pop. The *New York Post* still has sub-editors toiling over daily headlines, churning out the puns. One of my all-time favorites was on the front page: "Rums Felled," on the day President Bush accepted Donald Rumsfeld's resignation. "A Grave Shame" headlined a story about veterans not given proper burials. This pun is familiar to readers of *Romeo and Juliet*: the dying Mercutio describes his wound to Romeo, "No, 'tis not so deep as a well nor so wide as a church-door, but 'tis enough, 'twill serve. Ask for me tomorrow, and you shall find me a *grave* man." This example reminds us that puns have the power to stimulate even when the situation is not amusing. In fact, the pathos of the moment is heightened as Mercutio uses a play on words to reveal the gravity of his wound. Our mind perks up: "Which way is that word meant?" The jolt adds power to any scene. So it would be totally useless to be groaning inside while performing a scene with puns! Instead, be fueled with the charge the pun provides, *share* that with your audience, and let them have the experience, too.

Performed puns

Enacted puns are a great fun. Students prepare these as micro-performances for the class. We heighten the performative element of the sharing in order to increase the punch of the pun. An MC can introduce the performed pun with a title, such as "Giving me the cold shoulder." The performer steps out and puts ice cubes on her shoulder. Or you can opt to enact the pun first and announce the title afterwards, or even ask the audience to guess. For example, someone enters in a blue sheet, unfolds it and declares, "Out of the blue!" My favorite performed pun was by a student who stood in a doorway and threw a large handful of pennies and other coins into the room while saying, "The Winds of Change."

Performing puns can help you learn to leap more easily from a literal to metaphorical sense of a word, from one connotation to another. Groucho Marx as Rufus T. Firefly twists words mercilessly in the opening of *Duck Soup*. He plays to the unflappable doyenne, Mrs. Teasdale, managing to confound her serious intentions with wordplays on her every line (see www.youtube.com/watch?v=Dsw9jYU_rJI):

> Mrs. Teasdale: (*pompously*) As Chairwoman of the reception committee, I welcome you with open arms.
> Firefly: Is that so? How late do you stay open?
> Mrs. Teasdale: I've sponsored your appointment because I feel you are the most able statesman in all Fredonia.
> Firefly: Well, that covers a lot of ground. (*He looks her up and down*) Say, you cover a lot of ground yourself. You'd better beat it. I hear they're going to tear you down and put up an office building where you're standing. You can leave in a taxi. If you can't leave in a taxi, you can leave in a huff. If that's too soon, you can leave in a minute and a huff.
>
> (Kalmar and Ruby 1972)

Blunderings, mishearings, malapropisms, eggcorns, and mondegreens

Puns reveal the multiplicity of meanings that lurk beneath the surface. No longer can language curtail experience and a word signify only one thing. Mishearings, malapropisms, eggcorns, and mondegreens use the accidental or the inaccurate to undo words and their sense. Mishearing progressions (related to the childhood game of "Telephone") are built on sequences of four: three questions and an answer to the last question.

We form a circle, and the first person starts with a question. The second and third person both have to "mishear" the original question. The last person in the sequence answers the third question.

Need more Doritos?
Good for libidos?
Your favorite is Cheetos?
But don't double-dip!

Has spring really sprung?
Has the telephone rung?
Was the king really hung?
He was a ruler: 12 inches.

An audacious use of "mishearing" is the opening to the musical *Spamalot* (see www.youtube.com/watch?v=KoTR8sBGfyY). The plummy historian pontificates: "This man was the King of the Britons, for this was England." And the curtains open to a complete mock-folkloric song and dance number about Finland. It goes on for a while until the historian corrects the mishearing: "I said England." The company replies all together: "What? Oh, sorry, sorry about that." And the scene dissolves.

Mishearing develops the skills applicable for mondegreens (shortened from a mishearing of "laid him on the green," or Lady Mondegreen), words of text or song that have been misheard and replaced with something that produces a skewed sense. Adults often relate these mondegreens as adaptations of phrases they were asked to repeat as children but didn't understand. A famous example is the Pledge of Allegiance, the mondegreen version of which is, "I pledge a lesions to the flag." It is interesting to take a familiar text and write an alternative that sounds similar but is incorrect.

Eggcorns, earslips, and bloopers are slips of the tongue that arise out of ignorance or misspeaking. There are many collections of these spoken or written errors, passed virally and collected in books. In one recent workshop, a performer amazed us with a story. She had been in an unhappy marriage, and during a long car ride had read aloud with her husband the whole of *Anguished English,* a famous book of errors collected by Richard Lederer. It didn't save their marriage, but they laughed for many miles. Eggcorns (from a mishearing of acorn) are errors that are repeated until someone actually believes the incorrect version is correct: "for all intensive purposes," instead of "for all intents and purposes." The word malapropism comes from Sheridan's wonderful *mal à propos* (French for inappropriate) character from *The Rivals,* Mrs. Malaprop. She pretends to be versed in the cultural niceties, but makes verbal errors that expose her ignorance. "Sure, if I reprehend anything in this world, it is the use of my oracular tongue, and a nice derangement of epitaphs." Authors often give their characters slips of the tongue to reveal social insecurities. Shakespeare's characters such as Dogberry, Launcelot, Elbow, Juliet's Nurse, Armado, and Bottom all use this tactic, and we laugh at their errors. Collections of the verbal slips of Dan Quayle or George W. Bush rival any author's creation.

We explore blundering words by reading scenes with error-filled characters, and then, in pairs, create some of our own. One partner says a correct phrase and the other tries to make up a close error. We choose our best material to present to the group.

Actors do not always know how to *play* malapropisms. They can be heavy handed or pretend to be stupid, and *prevent* the audience from enjoying the error. After working to hear, understand, and create this group of blunders, we begin to appreciate how easy it is to make an error, and how to find the exact kind of error the character would make. The audience begins to share the performer's comic delight, which is how the error can illuminate a deeper truth. These new perspectives help actors' comic delivery of wrong-worded characters.

Free association

The last circle game I describe here takes us to one end of the wit-and-wordplay spectrum, where ordinary sense is overthrown by nonsense. The skill set students acquire with this game prepares them to play Fool characters, who destroy the common-sense world of the person with whom they are speaking. This is the domain of the Marx Brothers, the mad-dervish wit-makers. Harpo without words performs puns that mix the literal with the figurative. Groucho tangles language and logic and goes on wild non-sequiturs, often with Chico, who performs a variety of puns in fake Italian-accented English. Between them, they reduce whole groups of perfectly upstanding people to raving idiots.

We free-associate in a circle, using all of our skills: puns, mishearing, proverbs, rhyme, etc., bouncing off whatever has been offered by the previous player. And we don't have to wait for our turn, which ups the ante for mayhem.

> *(Picking dust bunny off the floor)* What are all these interesting things? They're metaphors. Dead metaphors. Petit-fours. The hair is actually from a meta-fur. It's an evergreen: a meta-fir. Say, can you hunt for a meta-fur? And will the meta-fur try to escape by climbing itself? My question is whether it's green all year, or whether it hibernates. Could it bear it, do you think? I met a fur-ry bear in the woods. I de-fer to you. I climbed a tree to escape him.

This is an open and free form. To paraphrase Salvador Dali, you have to create confusion systematically in order to set creativity free. A recent study suggests that exposure to things that are illogical can prime the brain for finding new patterns: "disorientation begets creative thinking" (Carey 2009).

Arriving at this point of nonsense brings us to the conclusion of the first part of our work. These games have given us the ability to hold and juggle complex thought and language, in a pleasurably swift and light way. The next part of the work is to move to the other end of the wit spectrum, where wit is condensed into epigrams, aphorisms, and chiasmus, those sophisticated pearls of wordplay.

Finally, we explore character types that embody wit, such as the fool and the rustic clown, to see how wit can be applied in social and political discourse. But we'll leave that for another day.

Why play with words?

People come to the theatre for an experience of live, vital language. Plays with wit and wordplay deserve to be delivered fully and with joyful expertise. If we don't necessarily use these skill-sets in our daily lives, we need to cultivate them. Dabbling with wit rubs off. Feedback after the first day of a workshop: "I feel as if I am firing on more cylinders than usual." "I feel freer." "I have a clarity and ability to make connections." After only a short exposure, students and audiences develop an ability to hear and appreciate wit and a desire to create and enjoy it themselves.

From our earliest giggling, babbling selves we get pleasure from playing with language. As we grow, we come to understand our world more deeply through the complexity that wordplay encourages. That enjoyment in wit, with the agility of thought it engenders, ultimately protects us from a rigid and reductive worldview.

> Freedom begets wit and wit begets freedom.
> (Jean Paul, *Introduction to Aesthetics*, 1804)

Acknowledgments

Deep thanks to all the students who have been exploring this work with me, and special thanks to the wondrously witty Hall Hunsinger, who has helped me greatly in developing this pedagogy.

References

Carey, Benedict. 2009. "How Nonsense Sharpens the Intellect." *New York Times*, October 3.

Carroll, Lewis. 1946. *Alice's Adventures in Wonderland*. New York: Random House.

Dobbs, David. 2013. "Playing for All Kinds of Possibilities." *New York Times*, April 23.

Erasmus, Desiderius. 1963. *On Copia of Words and Ideas*, translated and with an introduction by Donald B. King and H. David Rix. Marquette, IL: Marquette University Press.

Gordon, George. 1928. *Shakespeare's English*. Oxford: Clarendon Press.

Hill, Carl. 1993. *The Soul of Wit*. Lincoln, NE: University of Nebraska Press.

Kalmar, Bert and Harry Ruby. 1933. *Duck Soup*. Screenplay. In S. J. Perelman *et al.* (1972), *The Four Marx Brothers in Monkey Business and Duck Soup*. New York: Simon & Schuster.

Legman, Gershon (ed.). 1964. *The Limerick*. New York: Bell Publishing Company.

Sanches, Mary, and Barbara Kirshenblatt-Gimblett. 1976. "Children's Traditional Speech Play and Child Language." In Barbara Kirshenblatt-Gimblett (ed.), *Speech Play:*

Research and Resources for Studying Linguistic Creativity. Philadelphia, PA: University of Pennsylvania Press.

Shakespeare, William. 1974. *The Riverside Shakespeare.* New York: Houghton Mifflin.

Sheridan, Richard Brinsley. 1988. *The Rivals.* In Richard Brinsley Sheridan, *The School for Scandal and other Plays.* London: Penguin Books.

Stewart, Susan. 1978. *Nonsense: Aspects of Intertextuality in Folklore and Literature.* Baltimore, MD: Johns Hopkins University Press.

Stoppard, Tom. 1974. *Travesties.* New York: Grove Press.

8

COMEDY STRUCTURE AND ACTING CHOICES

Greg Dean

I've read dozens of books on theater, camera, and commercial acting, and they all had one shortcoming in common. They all stated that actors need to find the humor in the scene, but they never explained how to do it. This chapter will fill in this neglected area of acting. First, it'll explain basic joke structure, so you can find the jokes written into the script. Next, it'll lay out the categories of the behavioral actions: character, body language, physical action, emotion, state of mind, voice inflection, and sound effect. These will allow you to add humor to a script without changing the written word. And finally, it'll present a series of exercises so you can practice creating jokes using the techniques you've just learned.

The fact that all comedy and jokes have a basic structure in common is unknown to the general population. Most actors and comedians don't even know this. And even though humor and jokes are an ongoing concern for actors, most comedic acting choices are made by intuition and guesswork. Sometimes they're given to you by a director who understands comedy (if you're lucky). My aim is to give students a personal understanding of joke structure. This will enable you to find the jokes written into the script, and also to add behavioral jokes, and then perform them at will.

This chapter assumes that you have some acting training and already know the basics, such as analyzing scripts, choosing an intent for a scene, and knowing that *all acting choices are considered actions*. Therefore, these fundamentals will not be discussed here.

Joke structure

Let's start by challenging your belief system about jokes. *There's no other way to communicate comedy or humor than through jokes.* That's right, no other way. All comedy and humor has one basic structure. What you're about to learn is how comedy happens in the human mind. To aid this process, you must first let go of your traditional definition of the word "joke," and open your mind to a different paradigm.

Most people think jokes begin with, "These two guys went into a bar ..." or "Do you know the difference between ..." or "I don't get no respect ..." Yes, these are jokes, but so are all the funny things that happen naturally, things that aren't generally recognized as jokes, but which still make us laugh. These are the things about which people might say, "That's just funny." I am here to dispel the myth that these things aren't jokes too, and to show you that the structure of all humor is the same. It's joke structure.

Setup and punch

Traditionally, jokes contain two parts: setup and punch. The point of discussing setup and punch is to establish that all jokes require two parts. These two parts have different functions and effects on an audience. Let's begin with how setups work.

Setups

The setup's function is to create misdirection by getting the audience to buy into a false expectation. Take this setup written by my student Terry L. Jackson: "After my divorce I had a sex change." What do you think this means? If you're like most people, you assume he's had a transgender operation. This is exactly the desired effect this setup was designed to achieve. Terry knew exactly what he wanted the audience to falsely believe as a result of hearing this setup.

Next, let's explore how punches work.

Punches

The function of the punch is to contradict the setup's false expectation and surprise the audience. Here's Jackson's entire joke:

Setup: "After my divorce I had a sex change."
Punch: "From very seldom ... to not at all."

If you're like most people, this punch surprised you because the setup caused you to assume "sex change" meant *change in sex organs*, and then the punch contradicted this by making "sex change" mean a *change in sexual frequency*. This expectation and contradiction were deliberately used by Terry to craft and write this joke. When an expectation is contradicted, this surprise causes people to laugh.

Expectation and contradiction

Next, we'll focus on how *expectation* and *contradiction* relate to understanding jokes in scripts. To demonstrate this, here's a scene from the sitcom *The Mary Tyler Moore Show.* If you'd rather watch this clip, scan the QR Code to view it on your smart phone or tablet. Or go to youtube.com/gregdeancomedy (Great Comedy Examples playlist). If you don't have a QR scan app, go to Google and look for one. They are free.

In the episode, *Chuckles Bites the Dust,* a children's clown named Chuckles gets killed at a parade while dressed in the costume of his character Peter Peanut when a rogue elephant tries to shell him. This news starts Murray cracking a series of irreverent jokes. Mary is appalled and chastises everyone who laughs at these jokes.

In a later scene, all the members of the news station attend Chuckles's funeral. Murray makes more jokes and Mary continues to berate him and the others for laughing. As the funeral begins, the minister recounts the many characters played by Chuckles. To her horror, the absurdity of this whole situation pushes Mary into involuntary laughter. She fights her bursts of laughter until the minister says, "Excuse me, young lady. Yes, you. Would you stand up, please?" Mary stands. The minister continues, "You feel like laughing, don't you?" Mary stifles a laugh. The minister encourages her, "Go ahead, laugh out loud. Don't you see, nothing would have made Chuckles happier? He lived to make people laugh. Tears were offensive to him, deeply offensive. He hated to see people cry. So go ahead my dear, laugh for Chuckles." Mary crumbles into uncontrollable sobbing.

Here's a breakdown of the expectation and contradiction for Mary's character: When Mary disapproves of the jokes and laughter about Chuckles' death, we expect her to continue this same behavior at the funeral. She contradicts the disapproving behavior with uncontrollable bursts of laughter. When the minister encourages her to laugh, we expect her to laugh, which she contradicts, by crying.

Expectation and contradiction is a script analysis tool for identifying and/or constructing jokes in any scene.

Acting choices

Behavioral actions

Everything in acting is an action, which includes dialogue, intent, blocking, behaviors, etc. Next we'll look at behavioral actions in terms of expectation and contradiction. We'll do this in order to understand how to add jokes to the dialogue of any script without changing the written word.

Here are the behavior actions categories:

- character
- body language
- physical action
- emotion
- state of mind
- voice inflection
- sound effect.

Behavioral actions don't always fit neatly into a singular category. The categories I've introduced can overlap, because they're often interdependent. A character may be expressed using body language; a sound effect might reveal an emotion, and so on. My concern isn't that these acting choices fit into perfect categories, but rather that you understand how to use these choices to construct jokes.

Next, we'll define and give examples for all the behavioral actions.

Characters

Character refers to any character you can portray in a scene. The character acted out should be different than you in posture, voice, psychology, personality, nationality, race, age, dialect, etc. This category includes animals and things the actor can personify into a character, as well as impersonations. It's helpful if characters are famous, stereotypes, or archetypes, because these are associated with assumed traits, which can be used to create an expectation or contradict one.

These character portrayals can last a very long time, like in the movie *Tootsie*, where Dustin Hoffman played the character Michael, an out of work actor. To get acting parts, Hoffman's character Michael created the character Dorothy, a spunky older lady. There are many examples of this in movies such as, *Mrs. Doubtfire*, *Sleuth*, *Some Like it Hot*, and the list goes on.

 Conversely, a character can also appear and disappear in the flash of a line or gesture. Take, for instance, Tom Cruise, in *A Few Good Men*. Cruise plays the character Lt. Kaffee, a cocky young lawyer. If you'd rather watch this clip, scan this QR Code to view it on your smart phone or tablet. Or go to youtube.com/gregdeancomedy (Great Comedy Examples playlist).

In an intense scene, Cruise made the behavioral choice to mock the Jack Nicholson's character, Col. Jessup, by impersonating his voice. Doing a Nicholson/Jessup impression, Cruise says, "He eats breakfast 300 yards away from 4000 Cubans that are trained to kill him." This behavioral choice created a moment of comic relief.

The action of character can be a powerful and fun way to add behavioral jokes to any scene.

Body language

The category of body language refers to postures, gestures, and facial expressions; e.g., crossed arms, frowns, pointing, etc. This category should not be confused with a similar category of physical action. Physical action requires the body to interact or affect someone or something. For instance, shaking your fist at someone is body language, whereas punching someone is what we're calling a physical action.

Many years ago, I had a female student who was also a professional dancer. She did a routine about that, which included this joke:

I finally got work at Radio City Music Hall … as an usher.

Good joke. To improve the joke I suggested she say the setup posed like a Rockette's dancer. This pose created a stronger expectation that she had gotten work as a dancer. When she said the punch "as an usher" (which contradicted the setup's dialogue and the new pose), she got a much bigger laugh.

Jack Benny was the best at using takes and looks to get long sustained laughs. One of his best jokes is based on his famously cheap character being robbed. The robber pointed a gun at Benny and said, "Your money or your life." The expression on Benny's face caused a huge laugh. His body language told us he was struggling to choose between being killed or giving up his money.

Unfortunately, this is only available as a radio recording, so if you want to listen to it scan the QR code to bring it up on your smart phone or tablet. Or go to: youtube.com/gregdeancomedy (Great Comedy Examples playlist).

Another clip of Jack Benny you can watch for his mastery of body language jokes is his violin duo with the very famous Gisele MacKenzie. Scan QR code or go to youtube.com/gregdeancomedy (Great Comedy Examples playlist).

The expectation for this second bit is that Jack Benny should be the shining star of the *Jack Benny Show*. But when MacKenzie outplays him, his ego is threatened. He first reacts with looks, that is to say, body language. Then he chooses the physical action of playing more complex music. And finally he responds verbally. This is a great example of Benny's character flaws being expressed as behavioral jokes as well as verbal jokes.

Physical action

Physical action refers to the body's interaction with people or things, such as kissing, kicking a dog, driving a car, throwing a baseball, etc. The following illustration of making a joke using a physical action is not from a script, but from my life.

I was a clown with a traveling circus. Several of my friends and I stopped at a greasy-spoon diner full of truckers. The waitress was a twenty-something hottie who loved to flirt. She was wearing a halter top and a short skirt. She spoke loudly to get the attention of all the male truckers as she ate her fries during a break. At one point she said, "I need a napkin." As she put her knees on the stool and reached over the counter to get a napkin, her skirt rose and heaven appeared, framed by a thong. Being a comedian, I pulled myself out of the trance and looked around the room to find about thirty men frozen in mid-action, gawking at her perfectly round bottom. I held up my fork and dropped it on my plate with a loud clank. I chose a physical action to indicate that the sight was so good I could no longer hold my fork. This woke up everyone to the fact that we were all gawking at her backside, and the place went up in a roar of laughter. She blushed, ran into the back, and the truckers all laughed about how funny it was that someone had dropped his fork. This was a simple, everyday action, which in context broke up an entire restaurant full of diners.

Now I used the physical action of dropping my fork, which also caused a sound effect, but understand it was my physical action of dropping the fork on the plate that created the joke. Again, the border between body language and physical action can sometimes overlap and it doesn't matter as long as you get that laugh.

Emotion

Emotion is the expression of the actor's or character's feelings, such as love, amusement, anger, fear, worry, sadness, etc. Each emotion conveys certain expectations based on our past experience of reading those behaviors and understanding what they mean in context. For instance, if a man were to stomp around muttering about someone, you would expect him to hate that person. Then if he were to say, "That's what I get for being in love," that would contradict the expectation established by that Emotion. Yet it can still be an honest and believable choice.

An example I love is of Charlie Chapin using emotion to create expectation and reveal a contradiction is from his movie *The Idle Class*. Scan QR Code or go to youtube.com/gregdeancomedy (Great Comedy Examples playlist).

In this scene, Chaplin plays a wealthy drunkard in his parlor who finds a note from his wife. She's just informed him that she has left and will stay away until he stops drinking. He turns away from the camera, picks up a picture of his wife from the counter, and as he sets it down, he leans over. His shoulders begin shaking up and down spasmodically. He's sobbing, right? Nope. As he turns around, we see he's shaking up a drink in a martini mixer. He's perfectly content with his cocktail.

Chaplin's shaking shoulders created the expectation that he was crying, and the mixing of the drink contradicted it. Emotion is easy actions to create great comedy.

State of mind

State of mind refers to mental dispositions that are not emotions, for example: confused, stubborn, contrary, drunk, stoned, calculating, determined, etc. States of mind are terrific for creating expectations or contradicting them.

Here's an example of a state of mind acting choice from the classic Monty Python's Flying Circus sketch "Argument Clinic." Scan QR Code or go to youtube.com/gregdeancomedy.

In this sketch, Michael Palin knocks on the door where he's expecting to get an argument. John Cleese is his argument attendant. From the first word out of Palin's mouth Cleese argues with him.

Palin: If this the right room for an argument?
Cleese: I've told you once.
Palin: No you haven't.
Cleese: Yes I have.
Palin: When?
Cleese: Just now.
Palin: No you didn't.
Cleese: Yes I did.
Palin: Didn't.
Cleese: Did.
Palin: Didn't.
Cleese: I'm telling you, I did.
Palin: You did not.
Cleese: I'm sorry, is this a five-minute argument or the full half-hour?
Palin: Oh. Oh, just the five-minute one.

The rest of the sketch is a series of contradictions and arguments about whether mere contradiction is really an argument. Eventually an outraged and dissatisfied Palin leaves. This is a great example of using a state of mind (in this case of wanting to argue) to create expectation and contradiction.

Voice inflection

Here's what Wikipedia has to say about inflection. "In grammar, *inflection* is the modification of a word to express different grammatical categories such as tense, mood, voice, aspect, person, number, gender and case." Voice inflection is produced through tone, emphasis, speed, rhythm, and pauses.

To express sarcasm, actors use a voice inflection that would be more appropriate for conveying the opposite of what they're saying. One my favorite examples of using voice inflection to create a laugh was in the movie *Die Hard*, when Bruce Willis's character John McClane had been chased, beaten up, shot, and cut by glass.

He was hiding in an air duct and crawling to get away from the bad guys and said, "Come out to the coast. Get together. Have a few laughs." The voice inflection made it so clear he meant the opposite of what he was saying, and the effect was quite funny. Scan QR Code or go to youtube.com/gregdeancomedy.

Sound effect

Sound effect refers to the sounds actors can make with their mouths, bodies, or an object the character might carry or find. Sound effect includes almost any non-word sound an audience can hear and understand. Sound effect includes burps, mouth explosions, claps, footsteps, farts, whistles, dog barks, and so on.

Harpo Marx is one of the great examples for using sound effects to create jokes. Since Harpo's character didn't speak, he'd often whistle to communicate his message. His ability to whistle to communicate makes for some of the highlights of the Marx Brothers movies. If you haven't studied their movies, start now. They were unique because the scripts and gags were tested and improved on stage in front of a live audience before shooting them as movies. Scan QR Code or go to youtube.com/gregdeancomedy.

Sound effects also include what are called expressive interjectors. Injectors are the sounds we make, such as: shhh, hmmm, whew, ahem and so on. These injectors, if done right, aren't words, but rather vocal expressions of mood or intent. For instance, Lucille Ball was known for one particular interjector. Whenever she was caught in one of her many con schemes, she'd interject, "Uggh." I'm not sure if I spelled it correctly, but nonetheless she used it often to great comic effect. (I 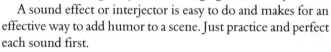often wondered how the writers wrote that action in the scripts.) Scan QR Code or go to youtube.com/gregdeancomedy.

A sound effect or interjector is easy to do and makes for an effective way to add humor to a scene. Just practice and perfect each sound first.

Summary

Once you understand the comedy structure of expectation and contradiction, you'll easily *find* the jokes written into any script. Then using the behavioral actions of character, emotion, state of mind, body language, physical action, voice inflection, and sound effect, you'll actually be able to *create* jokes where there are no jokes written.

By applying these acting tools, a whole new world of comedic possibilities will open up to you. As you begin to appreciate how the top comedic actors use them, often without even knowing it, you'll learn how to enhance your own ability to make people laugh. Then audiences will be saying to you, "You're just naturally funny." But we'll know the truth.

Behavioral jokes game

Instructions

Now that you understand the basic joke structure of expectation and contradiction and are familiar with the categories of behavioral actions, it's time to put all this into practice. We'll do this with a series of simple and fun games. Here's an example of how a game is laid out:

> **Dialog:** "I'm here for the cheerleader tryouts."
> *Behavioral expectations:*
> **Action category:** Character
> *Behavioral contradictions:*

These games all have several parts to them. In the first part, you'll list some behavioral expectations created by the dialog. These will be behaviors in the given action category for that particular game.

In the next part of the game, you'll write down behavioral contradictions for each of your listed expectations. And in the last part, you'll select one of your behavioral contradictions and along with the dialog act out a short scene to create a joke.

Altogether there are five discrete steps involved in playing the games:

1   Read the game's dialog and note the action category.
2   For this action category, list behavioral expectations created by the dialog.
3   List a behavioral contradiction for each expectation.
4   Select one of your behavioral contradictions.
5   Act out that behavioral contradiction along with the dialog in a short scene.

It sounds more complicated than it is, really. Let's play the same example game all the way through, and you'll see how easy and fun it can be.

1. Read the game's dialog and note the action category

> **Dialog:** "I'm here for the cheerleader tryouts."
> *Behavioral expectations:*
> **Action category:** Character
> *Behavioral contradictions:*

So here we're just going to notice that the dialog is "I'm ready for the cheerleader tryouts." And that the action category we'll be playing with is character (as opposed to sound effects, body language, sound effect, etc.).

2. For this action category, list behavioral expectations created by the dialog

Now we're going to list some of the character behavioral expectations. There's no need to be clever or funny. This step isn't meant to be funny. Just list some common or obvious expectations about a character who would say: "I'm here for the cheerleader tryouts."

For example:

> **Dialog:** "I'm here for the cheerleader tryouts."
> *Behavioral expectations:* It's a young woman, physically fit, cheerful …
> **Action category:** Character
> *Behavioral contradictions:*

3. List a behavioral contradiction for each expectation

Now, referring to your list of the behavioral expectations from step 2, list a behavioral contradiction for each of those expectations. In other words, for each behavioral expectation you listed, pick a character that contradicts that particular character in your behavioral expectation's list.

Here's what that might look like:

> **Dialog:** "I'm here for the cheerleader tryouts."
> *Behavioral expectations:* It's a young woman, physically fit, cheerful …
> **Action category:** Character
> *Behavioral contradictions:* male rapper, grossly obese, depressed …

4. Select one of your behavioral contradictions

Here you simply choose one of your behavioral contradictions that strikes you as funny when combined with the dialog.

> **Dialog:** "I'm here for the cheerleader tryouts."
> *Behavioral expectations:* It's a young woman, physically fit, cheerful …
> **Action category:** Character
> *Behavioral contradictions:* male rapper, grossly obese, depressed …

When I imagine an inner-city male rapper wanting to tryout to be a cheerleader, I see real possibilities for humor.

5. Act out that behavioral contradiction along with the dialog in a short scene

We now have all the makings of a behavioral joke. All that's left is to act out the dialog along with the behavioral choice. For instance, in this game you could now act out a scene as a male rapper walking in and saying, "I'm here for the cheerleader tryouts." Though the male rapper will have body language and vocal infections, these served to express the character. While we could debate how funny it is ... that's a joke. We came up with it just by playing this little game. Kind of cool, isn't it?

Right now, un-ass yourself from your Barcalounger and play this game on your own. Create your own behavioral expectations and behavioral contradictions and act out a scene to create a joke.

If one scene doesn't seem funny, then select another behavioral contradiction and act it out with the dialog to create a different joke. Feel free to experiment. Not all the choices you'll make will be funny. That's not the point. The point is to learn this technique for creating jokes within a script without changing the written word.

At the very end of this chapter you'll find a formatted page you can use to play your own games. Just write in a short line of dialog, and then pick one behavioral action category and write that in. Then do the five steps until you're acting out a short scene to make the joke come alive. For fun, see how many categories you can use with the same piece of dialog.

These games aren't meant for public performances, their purpose is to teach you the skill of making behavioral acting choices to create jokes. It' not important to follow the exact rules here... Just have fun playing these games. As you do, you'll come to understand behavioral jokes more and more, and soon you'll be able to create them whenever you want.

Appendix: practicing behavioral jokes

Game form 1

1   Read the game's dialog and note the action category.
2   For this action category, list behavioral expectations created by the dialog.
3   List a behavioral contradiction for each expectation.
4   Select one of your behavioral contradictions.
5   Act out that behavioral contradiction along with the dialog in a short scene.

> **Dialog:** "That is truly the best I can do."
> *Behavioral expectations:*
> **Action category:** Emotion
> *Behavioral contradictions:*

Dialog: "I'd like to introduce you to my mother."
Behavioral expectations:
Action category: Character
Behavioral contradictions:

Dialog: "It didn't affect me at all."
Behavioral expectations:
Action category: Body language
Behavioral contradictions:

Game form 2

1 Read the game's dialog and note the action category.
2 For this action category, list behavioral expectations created by the dialog.
3 List a behavioral contradiction for each expectation.
4 Select one of your behavioral contradictions.
5 Act out that behavioral contradiction along with the dialog in a short scene.

Dialog: "I'm so excited to be here."
Behavioral expectations:
Action category: Emotion
Behavioral contradictions:

Dialog: "I love walking on the beach."
Behavioral expectations:
Action category: Sound effects
Behavioral contradictions:

Dialog: "Your girlfriend/boyfriend seems very nice."
Behavioral expectations:
Action category: State of mind
Behavioral contradictions:

Game form 3

1 Read the game's dialog and note the action category.
2 For this action category, list behavioral expectations created by the dialog.
3 List a behavioral contradiction for each expectation.
4 Select one of your behavioral contradictions.
5 Act out that behavioral contradiction along with the dialog in a short scene.

Dialog: "Now, you can pour me some."
Behavioral expectations:
Action category: Physical action
Behavioral contradictions:

Dialog: "This is the best party ever."
Behavioral expectations:
Action category: Voice inflection
Behavioral contradictions:

Dialog: "This is the way I say good-bye."
Behavioral expectations:
Action category: Body language
Behavioral contradictions:

Game form 4

1 Read the game's dialog and note the action category.
2 For this action category, list behavioral expectations created by the dialog.
3 List a behavioral contradiction for each expectation.
4 Select one of your behavioral contradictions.
5 Act out that behavioral contradiction along with the dialog in a short scene.

Dialog: "It was an excellent meal."
Behavioral expectations:
Action category: Sound effect
Behavioral contradictions:

Dialog: "It's Miller time."
Behavioral expectations:
Action category: Character
Behavioral contradictions:

Dialog: "I am relaxed."
Behavioral expectations:
Action category: State of mind
Behavioral contradictions:

Game form 5

1 Read the game's dialog and note the action category.
2 For this action category, list behavioral expectations created by the dialog.
3 List a behavioral contradiction for each expectation.
4 Select one of your behavioral contradictions.
5 Act out that behavioral contradiction along with the dialog in a short scene.

Dialog: "I have to go now."
Behavioral expectations:
Action category: Body language
Behavioral contradictions:

Dialog: "Yeeeeha, y'all."
Behavioral expectations:
Action category: Voice inflection
Behavioral contradictions:

Dialog: "This should start a fight."
Behavioral expectations:
Action category: Physical action
Behavioral contradictions:

Blank form

1 Read the game's dialog and note the action category.
2 For this action category, list behavioral expectations created by the dialog.
3 List a behavioral contradiction for each expectation.
4 Select one of your behavioral contradictions.
5 Act out that behavioral contradiction along with the dialog in a short scene.

Dialog:
Behavioral expectations:
Action category:
Behavioral contradictions:

Dialog:
Behavioral expectations:
Action category:
Behavioral contradictions:

Dialog:
Behavioral expectations:
Action category:
Behavioral contradictions:

9

THE SECRET OF GREAT COMEDY

Scott Meltzer

What's the secret of great comedy? I'll give you a hint: It's not timing.

It's practice.

Whether you want to be a comic actor, a stand-up comedian, a comedy writer, or even a comedy juggler like me, your first hundred auditions, first hundred open mic nights, first hundred jokes, or first hundred street shows don't count. Don't even think about whether you're any good until after you've put in those first hundred, because in comedy everyone fails when they start.

Unlike other performing arts like dance, music, or even dramatic acting, in comedy you can always tell when you're failing. If they don't laugh, you've failed. And in every form of comedy, when first starting out, you fail a lot. Later, as you get more experience and more skilled, you still fail a lot, but you get more used to it.

I've been a professional comedy writer and comic performer for over three decades, and I still don't know how to sit down and write one funny joke. What I do know is how to write two dozen jokes and then find out which ones are funny. And this is how every comedy writer I know creates material: *volume*!

Some keep that process hidden and only pitch the jokes they think will work. Others vomit forth a non-stop stream of bad jokes until they hit the kernel of a germ of a seed of a decent idea. Either way, we all come up with far more losers than winners. Comedy writing is a numbers game, and most of the jokes you write will not be good.

That's okay.

It's hard to come up with a funny, new joke. It's not hard to come up with a lot of new jokes[1] and then pick the ones you think might be funny. After that, it's easy to find out if you're right. The audience will tell you loudly and clearly—or silently and even more clearly.

As you get more experienced, you will learn specific techniques and tools to make your gags better, but the most valuable thing you'll learn is how to come up with more bad gags faster.

Most of my comedy-writing and performing education came from doing thousands of street shows, trying out all kinds of bad jokes, and experimenting with different wordings and deliveries to try to improve them. (The rest of my schooling came from long car trips sitting on Greg Dean's lap, listening to his theories about target assumptions, context links, decoy assumptions, and connectors, but according to the terms of the settlement, I'm not allowed to talk about that except in therapy.)

The key is to not beat yourself up for all the bad jokes you write. Instead, you go onstage and try the few bits you think have some promise. Keep the gags that get laughs. Rework or cut the ones that don't.

Think of it as comedy Darwinism.

Comedy Darwinism

For Darwinian evolution to proceed, you need two things: random mutation and natural selection. When writing or performing comedy, the changes you make from show to show are the mutations. The audience's response provides the selection pressure.

Variety acts and stand-ups get to repeat the same material in front of multiple audiences, with the freedom to change whatever they want, and get the results of those changes immediately. Actors in movies and TV don't get this level of feedback or repetition, but they can still take advantage of power of comedy Darwinism.

In the documentary *Unknown Chaplin*, you can see a great silent-film comic using this process. Chaplin films his gags over and over, sometimes changing the smallest detail, before he's satisfied with the bit.

In the outtakes at the end the movies *Talladega Nights: The Ballad Of Ricky Bobby* and *Date Night* you can see the actors experimenting with dozens of different versions of the same gag, many of which were shown to test audiences before choosing which versions to include in the final movies.

Bert Lahr, a comic actor whose career spanned burlesque to Broadway, vaudeville to TV, and was best known as the Cowardly Lion in *The Wizard of Oz*, "worked hard on stage, trying out many different comedy gestures, eliminating the ones that did not get good laughs or which, in certain situations, killed a bigger one to come" (Lahr 1969: 45; 2013: 1101–1103).

Darwin's Theory of Comedy Evolution states that if all you did was just flop around onstage, keeping the gags the audience laughed at and cutting or changing gags when they didn't, eventually you'd have a show that got as many laughs as Charlie Chaplin, Will Ferrell, Steve Carell, Tina Fey, and Bert Lahr all put together.

Warning: this process could take another 4.5 billion years.

Intelligent design

If you don't have that kind of time, one alternative is intelligent design.

Many books and classes can teach you specific techniques to speed things up. There's even a chapter in this book on "Comedy Structure and Acting Choices" written by G–D Himself.

There are several rules-of-thumb that you can use to improve your gags. None of these are guaranteed to generate bigger laughs, and I can't tell you in advance which, if any, will work for a particular joke. Only the audience can do that. But the following guidelines will give you higher probability guesses and more useful experiments to try first.

When writing:

- Disguise your setup. Make it more natural, organic, important, informative, or inevitable. Make it something your character would say even if there weren't a punch line coming.
- Punch. Don't push. Make your punch line more extreme. Don't just break an assumption, *shatter it*!
- Choose one of the most commonly shared assumptions in the setup to shatter.
- Make your punch line shorter.
- Make your joke more specific.
- Don't write past the laugh. Put the reveal at the end of your punch line. (The reveal is the word or action that makes them start laughing.)

When performing:

- Pause and let the audience see you think. Let them share your thought process.
- Don't telegraph or anticipate your punch. Discover the punch at the same time as the audience does, or just before they do, or even just after—or deliver the punch without your character even knowing it's a joke.
- Don't talk past the laugh.
- Believe the assumptions your setup implies all the way up to the reveal.
- Raise the stakes. Make the setup matter a *lot* to your character.
- Be affected by the joke. Change your mind, mood, feelings, relationship, opinion, tactics, delivery, or status during the gag.
- Have a goal. Play the verb, not the adjective.
- Start at zero. One sure way to kill a joke is to expect the laugh you got last night.
- Find a strong reason for your character to say the line other than "because it gets a laugh."

Acting comedy

When you're writing material, this Darwinian process of making changes and testing them in front of an audience will be key to your survival. Even when you're not writing your own material, this same principle applies to your comedic acting choices.

As a comic actor performing another writer's dialog and jokes, it's hard to know in advance the timing, delivery, status, or emotions that will get the biggest laughs. Your director may have some opinions, and your ever-growing comic intuitions will give you clues, but only the audience can tell you for sure. There are, however, specific acting choices that are more *likely* to lead to bigger laughs, along with some common acting traps to avoid.

Believe and play the truth of your setup

One type of joke can be described as a logical statement taken to its illogical conclusion. For these lead-away jokes, your character should believe the truth of the setup, not the punch. You don't want to telegraph the punch with your acting. You want to lead away from it.

There's a joke old Jews tell about a Jewish man travelling through Texas. A Texan comes up behind the traveler and says:

Texan: (*Menacingly*) Are you a Jiiieewww?
Traveller: Why? Are you looking for a fight?!?
Texan: No. I'm looking for a Minyan.

I've seen this joke performed where the Texan's first line in the setup was done in a threatening Texas accent and the punch line was delivered with a Brooklyn Jewish accent. Logically this makes no sense. Why would the Texan hide his accent if he were looking for a fellow Jew? But comedically, it works perfectly. During the setup the audience is meant to believe the Texan is an anti-Semite trying to start a fight, therefore it's okay to play that truth until the punch line reverses it.

Shut up and let them laugh

Don't talk past the laugh. The reason for this is simple: When you keep talking after the audience starts to laugh, they will stop laughing so they can hear what you are saying. Do this enough times and you will train your audience to laugh less.

To avoid this problem when writing a joke, you want to structure your punch line so no more words come after the audience starts laughing. For example in this joke from my act:

Scott: We love performing for children, because … *(Pauses to look at Katrine for permission to say it)* … well because we can't have kids of our own.
Katrine: *(Starts to tear up and then, reacting to audience's "awwww," explains defensively)* No. No. It's not a biological thing. It's a court order.

We purposefully wrote the punch line so that it ended with the words "court order" instead of something like "It's a court order that prevents us from getting within 50 feet of them." We didn't want there to be any more words after the audience started laughing at "court order." We wanted to end with the reveal.

When performing a joke, you want to stop talking, even stop moving, when the audience starts to laugh. You don't want to distract them with anything that will stop their laughter. Bert Lahr made this comedy rule into law in his shows: "Never move on a joke. I can kill any joke by movement. It's disastrous" (Lahr 1969: 46; 2013: 1112). (An exception to this is when they're laughing at a physical action. Continuing that action will usually cause the laugh to continue and even grow. As a bonus, physical comedy allows you to add toppers during the laugh.)

As a stand-up comedian, you can just wait and bask in the laugh. You don't need any more motivation to freeze than that. As a comic actor, you want to find a reason for your character to hold for the laugh, a character-consistent motivation to be still and let the audience laugh. With the right joke, the longer you wait, the more they'll laugh.

Thug: This is a stickup! Now come on. Your money or your life.
Long pause leading to a big laugh.
Thug: *(Finally)* Look, bud, I said, "Your money or your life!"
Jack Benny: I'm thinking it over!

Experiment with different comic timings

There are two critical spots to time in a gag: How long you pause between the setup and the punch line and how long you wait after the punch. The time you wait between the setup and punch is called your "thought pause," while the time after the punch is called "holding for the laugh." Playing with the length and content of your thought pause can turn "ah ha" into "ha ha." Changing how long you hold for the laugh will affect the size of the laugh and the energy the scene gets going forward from it.

For example, in Alan Ayckbourn's *Comic Potential*, Chandler, the director of a bad soap opera, is complaining to his assistant, Prim, about one of the characters in the soap:

Chandler: She's a pain in the ass, this woman. Are we thinking of killing her off soon?
Prim: Certainly not. She's the most popular character …
Chandler: That figures. They always are, the ones I loathe.

(Ayckbourn 1999: 9)

Most productions get a strong laugh on "Are we thinking of killing her off soon?" and some get another, smaller laugh on "the ones I loathe." The difference between one laugh and two is usually caused by how well Prim times her line.

Classic joke timing would be for Prim to wait till the laugh on "killing her off soon" is about 2/3 to 3/4 of the way down from its peak before starting her line. This would have Prim cutting off the trailing laughs and final few giggles. If she airs the laugh out, waiting even longer, past the end of the last giggle, the moment will lose energy, but may gain focus. Which is better? That's for Prim to discover each night.

But we know that if Prim comes in too early, stepping on that first laugh, cutting it off prematurely, she will not only prevent it from growing as big as it could, she will also lose the second laugh. This is because a lot of the audience will won't hear her delivering the second setup. They'll miss her saying, "Certainly not. She's the most popular character" because they'll still be laughing at the first joke.

Chandler can also play with the length and content of his thought pauses.

1   The character already knows the punch while delivering the setup. This is how most sarcastic jokes are delivered. This is how David Spade performs most of his stand-up act. There is no thought pause because the character has the entire line in mind when he starts his setup. The character may still pause between the setup and punch to build tension in the audience, but the character is not discovering anything during that pause. He's relishing the punch to come.

2   Beat the audience to the punch. Here your character doesn't have the punch line in mind while delivering the setup. He needs to discover the punch. He thinks of it during the pause, just a breath before the audience does. In our example above, Chandler would think about how much of a "pain in the ass, this woman" is, and then pause just long enough to realize he has the option of killing her off.

3   Discover the punch at the same time the audience does. This is a wonderful timing when you get it right. During the setup, nobody knows where the joke is going. Not you. Not the audience. You all discover the punch line at the same time leading to a simultaneous explosion of comedy.

4   Discover the punch just after they do. This is more of a clown timing. Unlike the sarcastic comic who positions himself ahead of and smarter than his audience, this timing positions you just behind them, just a little slower than they are.

5   Never discover the punch. This is a full-on clown timing. Your character doesn't ever see the incongruity or contradiction inherent in the punch. Instead you deliver the joke with the full sincerity and belief in the assumptions of the setup. Only the audience sees how your punch actually shatters those assumptions.

In my and Katrine's act, we have a bit where two big, strong men from our audience attempt, and ultimately fail, to inflate balloons. Our dialogue after they fail is:

Scott: It's possible … just randomly … that they picked the two *(pointing toward the volunteers' uninflated balloons)* that were defective.
Katrine and Scott take the two uninflated balloons from the volunteers and quickly blow them up without any difficulty.
Katrine: It's possible … just randomly … that we picked the two … *(gesturing toward the two volunteers)* who were defective.

Katrine has lots of timing considerations here. First, she can get a laugh just by pausing long enough after she inflates the guy's balloon. The audience laughs at the fact that a middle-aged woman easily does something that a bigger, younger man couldn't. If her pause is too short here, she loses that laugh.

After that first laugh, she has yet another pause to play with. This is her thought pause between the end of the setup ("that we picked the two …") and her punch ("who were defective"). She has several timing options here. She can:

1 Deliver her line knowingly, sarcastically, pausing just to increase the insult.
2 Pause while gesturing toward the two volunteers just long enough to come up with the joke and "discover" her punch.
3 Time her pause so she delivers her punch ("who were defective") at the same time as the audience figures out that's where the joke is going.
4 Pause even longer, waiting for the audience to start laughing while she gestures towards the two volunteers, letting the crowd start to laugh as they figure out where the joke is going, and then getting an even bigger laugh when she finally takes them there. This is great timing to try when you have a laugh of confirmation (i.e. a laugh where the audience has already guessed what the punch line is going to be and is not waiting to be surprised by your punch). They're waiting for their guess to be confirmed.
5 Deliver the punch line without realizing she's pointing toward the volunteers at all. Instead, she thinks she's still referring to the balloons, not the volunteers, when she calls them the "two who were defective." The audience knows she's talking about the volunteers, but she innocently never does.

For this particular joke, in good shows, Katrine usually goes for timing #4. When we don't have as much focus, or the show isn't going very well, she speeds up and does timing #1 or #2.

Breaking down these timings is presented here only for analysis and description. Nobody thinks like this while they're performing, and few comics ever think like this at all. I envy them.

In performance, everybody times their jokes and pauses intuitively. Everybody does this by feel, but learning about other timing options expands your choices and gives you more ways to feel.

When you're playing with different timings, always experiment a few times with a pause that feels longer than natural. Longer pauses are not always better, but you'll never know how long you could pause until you've tried pausing too long. It's rare that an actor in a comedy will err on the side of pausing too long or going too slow (except maybe in a farce). The most common problems are the opposite.

Choose a more truthful motivation

The least interesting reason for a character to do something onstage is "because it gets a laugh."

The writer writes the line because she thinks it's funny. The director sets the blocking to make sure the sightlines are good. The drummer looks up from his newspaper to prepare for a rim-shot.

But you, the actor, should deliver the line not because it's funny, but because your character believes it. Your character has no expectation of a reaction, even after 500 performances, each with a huge guffaw at that exact same moment.

A great comic actor and my favorite improv teacher, William Hall, explained it to me like this:

> A novice actor asks an older, more experienced actress why he's no longer getting the big laugh he used to on the line, "Pass the salt."
>
> She replies, "Perhaps it's because you're asking for the laugh instead of asking for the salt."

This mistake, expecting the laugh you got last night, is one of the most common reasons why a joke that works one night falls flat the next.

Why was Jack Benny pausing so long when he was threatened with "Your money or your life?" Was it because the longer pause got a bigger laugh? Not a chance. He was actually thinking it over. He was playing the reality of the joke.

Make your gags real

Stand-up comics and variety acts get bigger laughs with gags that appear less planned and more ad-libbed. Comedians want the audience to forget there's a script.

As an actor, you rarely want your audience to think you're ad-libbing. You don't want them distracted, thinking about whether or not you've gone off script. You do, however, want them to forget they're watching a play. You want them to forget you're acting. When the audience suspends their disbelief and fully enters the world of the play, they laugh more.

That's why you want to do everything you can to keep them inside that world.

Live inside the play

When a comedy is dying, inexperienced actors often jump ship. They do little things to let the audience know that they also know the show isn't funny. They stand next to their characters, instead of living inside them. They wink as a way to save face and say, "Hey I know this crap isn't working too."

Some actors wink even when the show is going well, as if to tell the audience: "Look at how funny and clever I am." But whether an actor winks to protect his ego or to stroke it, winking damages the reality of the play. Winking may feel better, but it never works better.

The same goes for mugging. The overly exaggerated facial and hand movements some actors use to emphasize a joke undermine the rest of the show. Mugging often gets a laugh, but only by reminding the audience that they're watching a performance. This destroys the suspension of disbelief so necessary for theater.

One way to know if you're mugging is to ask yourself: Is the audience laughing at me the performer or at my character? Whenever the audience laughs at you, the actor, they lose a bit of their connection to your character, to your pathos, and to the drama of the play. Along with hurting the play, this can also diminish the better, deeper laughs to come.

An actor can often get a laugh from breaking character, physically or verbally commenting on the audience's lack of response. A dying joke creates tension and acknowledging its death can relieve that tension and generate a laugh. But you sacrifice the integrity of the character and the play whenever you make that choice.

Actors need to trust the script. Not because the script is always good, but because distancing yourself from it makes the show worse.

It's different when a stand-up comic comments on a joke dying. The reality of the stand-up's world is that she's a person onstage telling jokes. Honestly dealing with the audience's reaction to those jokes *is* living inside that reality.

But for a comic actor, that's not the reality you want to portray. You don't want the audience to see an actor performing in a play. Your reality should be the reality of your character, living in a real world that just happens to be on a stage with an audience seated invisibly behind a fourth wall. Your character doesn't know or care whether the invisible people behind the wall are laughing or not. Unlike a comedian, when an actor holds for a laugh, she holds in character.

Rehearse more effectively

Take advantage of the freedom of the rehearsal process to explore as many different options as possible. That's what rehearsals are for! Trying different deliveries and different versions of a joke in rehearsal may not be as informative as it would be in front of an audience, but it's safer, and sometimes it's all you've got.

Use your director and your growing comic intuition as your audience. Imagine you've got an audience watching while you rehearse. Pause for their imaginary laughs. And while you're at it, make them a great audience. Imagine you're killing! There's no reason to spend your rehearsal time with a bad audience in your head.

I heard a story (or maybe I made it up; I'm 53; there's no way to tell the difference anymore) about Marcel Marceau giving a master class in mime. He asked a student to perform a new routine, and it died. Totally tanked. The class hated it, and the student hated it even more. After it was over, Marceau's only instruction was: "Do it again, only this time as if it were good."

It was much better the second time.

Just try something different

Different isn't always better, but better is always different.

If you're the writer, try restructuring your joke using a different format. For example: try a rule-of-three format. (There's a good reason this is the most common joke format. You have to first make a pattern to break a pattern, and two similar things make the shortest pattern for you to break with a third.)

From *The Simpsons*:

> Reverend Lovejoy: Homer, There is goodwill in people of all faiths, whether they be *(looks at Flanders)* Christian, *(looks at Krusty)* Jew, or *(looks at Apu)* Miscellaneous.

Or from comic Laura Kightlinger:

> I can't think of anything worse after a night of drinking than waking up next to someone and not being able to remember their name, or how you met, or why they're dead.

If your gag is already in rule-of-three format, try it as a two-beat or just go straight to your punch.

What if Lovejoy had said:

> Homer, There is goodwill in people of all faiths, whether they be *(looks at Flanders)* Christian or *(looks at Apu)* Miscellaneous."

Or Kightlinger tried:

> I can't think of anything worse after a night of drinking than waking up next to a stranger, trying to remember why they're dead.

Would their laughs be smaller? Only the audience can say.

Sure, basic humor theory tells us that three is generally the best number of beats for a joke, but that's not always true for every joke. The only way to find the funniest format for your joke is to experiment.

Maybe your joke would work better as a riddle:

> Which is worse? Waking up next to an ugly stranger … or under a really sexy corpse?

What about reversing it or exaggerating it? Can you structure it as a call back, or an act-out, or as a tag for another gag? You'll never know which format will work better till you try a bunch of them.

When performing, try the gag with a different attitude or feeling: high status, low status, intelligence, stupidity, innocence, malevolence, anger, frustration, guilt, joy, confusion, lust, love, contrition, confidence, embarrassment, surprise, superiority, elation, relief, exasperation, jealousy, or regret.

Try the gag with a different motive: to please, to threaten, to insult, to be loved, to be seen as superior, to be respected, to impress, to undermine your partner, to flirt, to reveal, to conceal, to confide, to clarify, to excuse.

Try the gag as a different character. Experiment with different timings. Emphasize different words. Change the length or content of your thought pause. Try it smaller. Try it bigger. Whisper it. YELL IT! Make it a secret. Tell it to the world!

Make it more sarcastic. If that doesn't work, try more sincere. Change it from a criticism to a defense. Act it out rather than just telling it.

Perform the gag onstage. See how it works. Go home and think of a way to improve it. Go back onstage and try that. Repeat until hilarious.

Two examples

Flo Ziegfeld never wanted *The Ziegfeld Follies* to go more than a couple of minutes without a pretty girl onstage. So when W. C. Fields was performing in *Follies of 1918*, Flo sent a gorgeous dancer walking a Russian wolfhound across the stage in the middle of Fields's golf act. Fields ad-libbed: "That's a very beautiful horse" and got a big laugh.

But Fields wasn't satisfied. "I experimented night after night to find out what animal was the funniest. I finally settled upon, 'That's a very beautiful camel'" (Curtis 2003: 126; 2011: 2620–2621). Fields later immortalized this gag in his movie *The Golf Specialist*. And just to put myself in the same paragraph as W. C. Fields, here are just a few of the different versions of one joke from my act. The original version of the joke, performed with my first juggling partner, John Park, was:

Scott: Try this one. I call it: "The Pirouette!"
Scott shows off by throwing three knives to John and spinning around before John throws them back.

John: The pirouette.
John does the same trick back at Scott.
Scott: The double pirouette!!
Scott tops John by spinning twice before the knives come back.
John: The pirouette!
John proudly goes back to the easier, safer single spin trick.

The first time we did it, it got an okay laugh so we kept it in. Later, we tried it as a rule-of-three instead of a four-beat joke, and it got an even bigger laugh:

Scott: Try this one. I call it: The Pirouette!
John: The pirouette.
Scott: The double pirouette!!
Scott does one spin, and then foolishly stops mid-spin as John is about to throw a knife at him.
Scott: Wait!
Scott finishes his second spin.

Years later, with my current partner, Katrine Spang-Hanssen from Denmark, we added:

Scott: Try this one, my little Danish pastry. I call it: The Pirouette!
Katrine: I will, my day-old bagel. The pirouette!
Scott: Okay. The *double* pirouette ... *Wait!*

The extra words were cute, but the extra laughs were small. So we tried an even longer version:

Scott: Try this one, my little Danish pastry. 'Cause she's from Denmark. That makes her a Danish. I call it: The Pirouette!
Katrine: I will, my day-old bagel. 'Cause he's from New York. He's old, and no one wants him even at half price. The pirouette!
Scott: The *double* pirouette ... *Wait!*

This worked even better, with solid, extra laughs on "bagel" and "half price." But I wanted to find one more laugh, so I tried:

Scott: Try this one, my little Danish pastry. Cause she's from Denmark. That makes her a Danish. That, and because sometimes she's filled with cream.

The audience hated it and hated me for it. Does that mean it was a mistake? Maybe. Did it hurt the routine? Sure. Did it kill the show? Not in the least. It just made the next 30 seconds a bit awkward. But telling the story to all my friends led BeeJay Joyer to suggest:

Scott: Try this one, my little Danish pastry. Cause she's from Denmark. That makes her a Danish. That, and because she's available till 10:00 every morning at Motel 6.

He's my hero.

We've tried the joke with me accidently failing to spin fast enough, failing on purpose, and not even trying. I've said "wait" as a command, a plea, a safe-word. I've yelled it, whispered it, used up-speak. We've spent years playing with this one little moment, and we're still not finished with it.

These little experiments always teach me something. And sometimes, just sometimes, one of the changes stays in our show.

The audience will tell you (almost) everything you need to know

Here's how Louis C. K. explained it:

> I remember seeing an interview with Jackie Gleason … where he said: "You can't do comedy without an audience, 'cause the audience tells you what to do. The audience tells you if it's funny. The audience tells you how long to sit with it. The audience tells you how to say it."
>
> (Maron 2014: t1:36:25)

The audience will tell you which jokes work and which don't. They will tell you with their laughter and with their silence, or worse with their coughs. They will tell you which delivery works best for which jokes. They will tell you how long to pause after the setup and how long to wait after the punch.

But they won't tell you why.

As a comic actor, you want to find legitimate, character-consistent reasons to make these more effective comic choices, and again, "because it gets a bigger laugh" is the least interesting reason I can imagine.

The audience is always right, except when they're wrong

The audience will teach you to be better, but they can also teach you to be worse. If the audience isn't laughing, you know something is wrong. When they do laugh, the takeaway isn't always as simple.

They will tell you that it's funny when you mug or break character, but they won't tell you how much this takes them out of the play and destroys the drama, as well as the comedy, for the rest of the show. They don't know that there are better jokes still to come in the reality of the play.

If you're a comedian, the audience will teach you to pander and be a hack. (Hack comes from the word "hackneyed" and refers to comics who recycle overused premises or steal other comics' jokes.) The audience will laugh at many things that will limit your future career. If you steal jokes, you will never learn to write them. If your material is based on premises others have already mined and you offer no new angles or insight, you make yourself generic.

The stand-up/Stanislavsky spectrum

Every comic character falls somewhere along a spectrum from stand-up comedian at one end to Stanislavsky-trained, method actor at the other.

The stand-up comedian knows she is being funny and understands the jokes she's telling. She delivers her jokes directly to the audience, and the audience is always aware of her performance. The comedian acts as the narrator of jokes and stories, most often told in the past tense. When she acts out the characters in her joke, they are like a mask. The audience remains fully conscious of the performer playing these short-lived roles.

The comic actor fully inhabits and disappears into her characters. The performer melts away leaving the audience seeing only the character. When she delivers a laugh line, she never does it to make the audience laugh. (Even in comic soliloquy she is not delivering jokes to the audience as much as she is confiding in them or talking to herself.) Her character is not aware of the audience or the laugh, yet she still finds a way to follow many of the same comic rules as the stand-up:

- Don't move on a laugh.
- Don't telegraph the punch.
- End with the reveal. Don't talk past the laugh.
- Believe the assumptions your setup implies all the way up to the reveal.
- Punch, don't push.
- Pause and let the audience see you think.
- Start at zero.
- Be affected by the joke.

In the Rowan Atkinson TV comedy *Blackadder*, the eponymous Blackadder is closer to the stand-up end of this spectrum than Baldrick or Percy because Blackadder knows when he's being funny. Percy and Baldrick never do. Ralph Cramden is more stand-up than Ed Norton. When Richard Pryor did his longer act-outs, he performed them more like an actor than a stand-up. The Porter in *The Scottish Play* (for those of you who are superstitious, it's called *Macbeth*) is a stand-up comic who just happens to be hanging out with a bunch of actors.

In comedies of wit by authors like Oscar Wilde and Noël Coward, many of the lines are delivered by characters whose intent is to be funny and clever. These jokes can be delivered for the audience like a comedian, but I claim the play will be better if you deliver them to the other actors, as if they're the people your character is trying to be funny for.

Musical comedy is often played broader and shallower than drama, with more mugging and winking, but it doesn't have to be. You get to choose where on the spectrum you want to place your character, and the audience will tell you what they think of that decision.

Comic actors can learn a lot from comedians and vice versa. Comedians can learn to engage their audiences more and get bigger laughs by making the characters in their act-outs more fully formed and three dimensional, the way an actor would. And actors can get bigger laughs with a two-drink minimum.

Conclusions and confusions

Learning about comedy is not the same as learning to do comedy. If you want to be funnier onstage or off, there is no substitute for experience. Practice, practice, practice.

There are rules-of-thumb that can guide you. There are tips and techniques that can speed up the process. There are guidelines that can steer you away from the most common traps. I've attempted to present a few of my favorites in this chapter, but there's only one rule that I truly believe: Practice, practice, practice.

There are many theories about what makes something funny including:

* *the superiority theory* – attributed to Plato, Aristotle, and Hobbes;
* *the incongruity theory* – supported by Beattie, Koestler, Kierkegaard, and Kant;
* *the relief theory* – proposed by Spencer and Freud; and
* *the joke diagram theory* – insisted on by Dean, Dean, Dean and Dean.

Understanding these can help you create new gags and improve your performance of existing ones, but the only sure-fire way to get funnier is to get in front of an audience and practice, practice, practice.

You will find contradictory opinions and advice both within this book and even within this chapter. Comedy is like that. It's filled with contradictions. The rules of comedy are not written in stone. Otherwise this book would be way too heavy.

For every rule in comedy, there could be a great joke that breaks it. Comedy is all about breaking expectations and shattering assumptions, and every supposed comedy rule sets up an expectation that some joker can shatter with a laugh:

Bobcat Goldthwait: My wife is so fat …
Audience: How fat is she?
Bobcat Goldthwait: She's real fat. I don't have a joke for everything, you know.

Note

1 For specific tutorials on joke writing I suggest Greg Dean's *Step by Step to Stand-Up Comedy* and my online articles at *www.comedyindustries.com/columns*.

Bibliography

American Dream Comedy Team. 1980–1995. Comedy juggling act. Performance.

Ayckbourn, Alan. 1999. *Comic Potential*. London: Faber & Faber.

Benny, Jack. 1948. "Your Money or Your Life." *The Jack Benny Program*, NBC, March 28. See www.youtube.com/watch?v=p_XkdmRkOL0&t=25m35s.

Comedy Industries. 1999–present. Comedy Juggling Act. Performance.

Curtis, James. 2003. *W.C. Fields: A Biography*. New York: A.A. Knopf.

Curtis, James. 2011. *W.C. Fields: A Biography*. epub produced by Kimberly A. Hitchens. Kindle.

Date Night. 2010. Dir. Shawn Levy. 20th Century Fox Home Entertainment.

Dean, Greg. 2000. *Step by Step to Stand-up Comedy*. Portsmouth, NH: Heinemann.

Goldthwait, Bob. 1988. Meat Bob: Bob Goldthwait Live in Concert. Chrysalis. CD.

The Golf Specialist. 1930. Dir. Monte Brice. RKO Radio Pictures. See www.youtube.com/watch?v=wfm8gR12hA4&t=18m10s.

Kightlinger, Laura. n.d. Stand-up comedy act. Performance.

Lahr, John. 1969. *Notes on a Cowardly Lion: The Biography of Bert Lahr*. New York: Alfred A. Knopf.

Lahr, John. 2013. *Notes on a Cowardly Lion: The Biography of Bert Lahr*. Open Road Media. Kindle.

Maron, Marc. 2014. "Louis C. K. from 2010." *WTF with Marc Maron*, December 15. Podcast.

Meltzer, Scott. 2012–2015. *Be Funnier with Scotty Meltzer*. International Jugglers' Association and Scott Meltzer. See www.comedyindustries.com/columns.

Meyer, George. 1992. "Homer the Heretic." *The Simpsons*, October 8. Dir. Jim Reardon. 20th Century Fox Home Entertainment.

Scotty & Trink. 2005–present. Comedy juggling act. Performance.

Talladega Nights: The Ballad Of Ricky Bobby. 2006. Dir. Adam McCay. Sony Pictures Home Entertainment.

Unknown Chaplin. 1983. Dir. Kevin Brownlow and David Gill. Thames Television. January 5.

10

UNEXPECTED

5½ rules to better improvisation

Shad Willingham

So you want to be a better improviser. Well, that's not so hard to do. There's no shortage of improvisation classes in major cities throughout the United States and some smaller cities, too. Everywhere you turn there is a studio or school ready and willing to introduce you to the amazing and challenging world of improvisation. From Seattle to Chicago to Los Angeles, NYC and Toronto you can find a school tailor made for you. There are famous schools which churn out skilled improvisers as well as new up-and-comers who are pushing the envelope of structure and style. There are several famous companies you may have heard of because their alumni have achieved a great deal of success and notoriety. Groups like The Groundlings in Los Angeles and The Second City in Chicago, Upright Citizen's Brigade in NYC, BATS Improv in Seattle, Washington Improv Group in DC and Philly Improv Theatre in Pennsylvania (PHIT), to name a few. For each of these more famous and successful professional organizations there are dozens of lesser-known groups who are out there striving to make a name for themselves. Groups like Bovine Metropolis Theater in Denver, Jet City Improv in Seattle, The Brave New Workshop Theatre in Minneapolis, Coalition Theater in Richmond, Virginia, Bay Cities Improv Company in Mobile, Alabama and the list goes on and on. In addition to the dozens and dozens of professional and semi-professional groups all across the United States, you will find improv and sketch clubs at most major universities around the country doing their own thing.

In addition, these myriad performance troupes practice any number of different, yet related, styles of improvisation. From long-form to short-form, improv jam, Theatresports, the always elusive "Harold" and even Guerilla Improv. Along with these divergent styles there have been many, many famous improv teachers who have helped to shape the landscape of improvisational acting in this country. Teachers like Del Close, Gary Austin, Viola Spolin and Paul Sills, Dick Chudnow, David Shepherd, Keith Johnstone and those fellows from the Upright Citizen's Brigade, Matt Besser, Ian Roberts, and Matt Walsh.

In the olden days improvisational actors used to be outliers, performers on the fringe of legitimate theatre and the world of comedy. Even after improvisational actors broke through to the small and big screen it was still an art form that seemed to elude most actors. Eventually, the students and actors who learned their techniques from many of the groundbreaking companies and teachers began to spread their knowledge as performers, directors and instructors and the world started to see the great worth in the skills developed and possessed by the improv actor. Skills like spontaneity and a unique creativity. Good improv actors always have ideas and that's what director's want from their actors – ideas. Playwrights too sought out the assistance of the improv actor to develop new works and workshop ensemble-based projects. Skilled improvisers are unafraid. They jump in with vigor and they are always willing to go to that place in their art that is uncomfortable, forbidden or even just plain silly. They are interested in process as much as product and they love to play. Finally improvisation has permeated all aspects of the professional world in (and out) of show business. We find improvisation used in advertising. Commercial casting directors are often looking for experienced improvisers. Indeed, there are entire commercial calls that request only those actors who are experienced in improv. Often there are commercials which have no text written. Instead they rely on the actor to bring their own inventiveness to create the copy for the commercial. Agents are much more likely to be interested in a new actor if they have improvisation training on their resume. Just as it is important too for the stage actor to be classically trained, it is likewise important for the comedic actor to have a foundational expertise in improvisation and its structure. There are companies of actors who teach improv to business professionals to help them to better think on their feet and prevent the editing of their own ideas and improvisation has been used in law schools to teach students to stand in front of an audience and express themselves without appearing weak or vulnerable. The art form of improvisation has come of age and its applications are limited only by our imaginations.

Why am I telling you this? Well, the reason is that if you have a sincere desire to become an improvisational actor and you are serious about the amount of hard work and hours of failure, humiliation and having the most fun you'll ever have on the stage then you must, absolutely must, find yourself a theatre or school that teaches the foundational "rules" of improvisation. Only after you are experienced with the basic structure of successful improvisational storytelling can you flourish and blossom into a skilled, multi-faceted and spontaneous improv-er. For the purposes of this chapter I am going to assume that you have, at least, a working knowledge of the rules of improvisation, because, frankly, it is impossible to learn the craft of improvisation by reading a book. But you can, and I really believe this, be inspired to become better at something you already understand and have a passion for. That is why I've written this chapter, to encourage you to begin doing it or to keep doing it. To continue moving forward and practicing and playing and experimenting and failing beautifully and doing it again and again and again.

I personally believe that the greatest pursuit in the world is to bring joy to others through entertainment. Improvisation has the power to do that. Never forget that.

So here are some of my rules to be a better improviser. Or as I tell my students: Do these things to suck less.

1. Fail big

Stephen Sondheim once said "If you're going to fall on your face, you might as well fall from the top rung of the ladder." Alexander the Great said "Fortune favors the bold." And William Shakespeare said "Yo girl, take a selfie with me." The point is there is no success in anything without failure first. Except skydiving. When you set out to take your first step in life I promise you that you fell down. No one ever picked up a baseball bat and hit a home run. This is why we take swimming lessons and why the pogo stick can be so deadly. Don't mistake me. I do not wish you to be a failure. On the contrary, I want you to succeed fabulously.

What I'm speaking to is a shift in thinking. It's hard for us to embrace failing. For years you were likely told that failure is bad. No parent wants to see an "F" on their child's report card and these days you can't help but go online and see some viral video entitled "Epic Fail" only to see someone falling on their face. Literally. No, it's not easy, but you must welcome failure with a generous heart and a thick skin.

You must jump up, jump in, and risk. There can be no hesitation in your actions and no concern for the result. A few ways to do this are:

- Breathe.
- Don't try to be funny. Especially in the beginning. Play the character and create the story no matter where it goes.
- Make it all about your partner. Don't be a ball hog. Give and take, as they say. Be the best partner you can be and everyone will want to work with you.
- Listen, listen, listen. Get out of your head and put your attention on the person standing across from you. Be attentive, responsive, and available. (See above)
- Don't worry. What's the worst that can happen? I mean, we're not splitting the atom here – we're creating art. When did we start caring so much about looking foolish? When you were in elementary school you didn't care. You jumped in and out of reality with a finger snap. Do that now. Give yourself permission to abandon reality and ignore those concerns about

preconceived notions and the perceptions of others. You can play make-believe again… as long as you follow the rules.

When you stop focusing on being good and start focusing on being present, things will begin to change. Every time you get up you will get better. When you accept that failing is part of succeeding, your choices will start to be more creative and your performance will become more interesting. When you stop worrying about being right you start to bring yourself to the work and who you are is what will make your choices so much more compelling and unique. The Buddhists say life is suffering. The same is true with improv. Until it's not.

2. Fun = fun

One of the greatest minds ever to come out of The Second City in Chicago (along with Bill Murray and John Belushi) was the gifted writer and director Harold Ramis. He is credited with saying that "Good actors make it look easy. *Great* actors make it look fun." I have taught acting and improvisation classes for years and each semester I am regularly stunned by the number of people who take my course and say that what they want more than anything is to be performers. Yet every time I call out an exercise or game the same 6 or 7 students jump up or raise their hand. These few brave souls are the actors who are excited about performing and actually enjoy the experience of being up there and taking part. The other 14 or 15 students have to be encouraged or cajoled into volunteering. Some of them honestly seem as hesitant as if they were walking to the dentist.

If we agree that you must fail to succeed (and we do) then we must also agree that you cannot succeed from your chair over there in the corner. You want to get better? You want to get good at this very specialized and marketable skill? Then get on your feet and do it. Oh yeah, and have fun. And while you're at it have a good time getting that root canal. Now no one knows better than me how hard it can be to get up there and put your ass on the line, but if you want success, it's the necessary step.

The reason performers feel this way is very simple. They are scared. They are afraid of looking silly or stupid. They're worried that they'll be bad and people will judge them. Well, that's too bad. I can promise that people will think less of you if you don't participate. The reward of success as an improvisational actor will not, ever never, come to you if you don't want to be on the stage. You will quit. You will give up and walk away. I swear it's true. So you must find the joy in training and performing. You must find a way to enjoy the doing of improvisation. Because when you are having fun, the audience is way more likely to enjoy themselves. Have you ever been in a play or performance and someone came up to you afterward and said something like "you look like you were having so much fun"? That's a good thing.

So, if you're one of these people who glue themselves to their seat during improv class, how do you change this hesitant behavior?

Fake it til you make it.

Yeah. It's that easy. And it works. Basically you must delude yourself into believing that you're having fun. And the strange thing is that if you do this every time, you will actually start to enjoy yourself. It's like muscle memory. In time your memory takes over and you start to have fun. Keep getting up and keep up the act.

Honestly, it doesn't matter how you get there. But if you cannot find a way to bring a lightness and a positivity to your work I wouldn't hold out much hope. Just remember, the difference between a good performance and a great performance, is the joy of performing. Find what it is about being on stage that makes you happy or satisfied or excited or titillated and focus on that thing. Remind yourself why you took that class or that you want to make people laugh or that you lost a bet and let that guide you. You will get there but it takes practice and practice and more practice to be fearless and joyful on the stage.

3. Irony anyone?

When watching an experienced improvisational actor it is immediately evident that they make choices that are unpredictable. This, like any other aspect of improv training is a learnable skill. Some performers are initially better at it than others but you can improve. You can get better. Stereotypical or cliché choices are to be expected in the beginning. We live in a world of watchers and copycats. Now, you may have heard that imitation is the highest form of compliment, and there's something to that. As a society, we consume so many images and videos that we have begun to consciously or unconsciously duplicate the work of others. In many cases I see actors looking to steal as much as they can, thereby stripping away their individuality. I have witnessed student actors of mine go to Youtube immediately upon being cast in a show to see if there's some video of another production of the same play to check out how someone else played their role. This is a terrible idea. First and foremost it kills almost any personal creativity you might bring to the part. It also robs your collaborators of the opportunity to craft a performance together with you. You simply cannot un-see the images from that video and therefore it will inform every choice you make from that point forward.

Invariably an actor's first ideas will be their most predictable choices anyway. It's not until you encourage actors to try new things and make new choices and you get to choice number 3 or 4 that a performers true creativity begins to appear. Therefore, I urge you not to spend too much time watching others on video or online. Working in a studio with classmates or in an improv troupe with other performers is your way to success. In those situations you are honing and sharpening your skills alongside others who, presumably, have the same general experience level as you. You want to watch videos entitled "Epic Fail," that's up to you, but try to stay away from watching others for ideas or to learn how to do it "better."

When I work with beginning and intermediate improvisational actors I always encourage them to use irony as a way to sharpen their skills of unpredictability. What is irony?

Well, the dictionary defines irony thus:

> The expression of one's meaning by using language that normally signifies the opposite, typically for humorous or emphatic effect.

What does *that* mean? For our purposes what it means is go in the opposite direction when you're making an acting choice in an improvisational sketch. Easier said than done I know, but if you make it part of your practice it will pay off. You will begin to see the opportunities to make converse decisions in your acting. Here is an exercise that can sharpen your ability to go in an opposite direction using irony and having fun doing it.

In "What Can I Do For You" two performers get up. Performer A remains in the space while Performer B prepares to enter. The purpose of B entering is to be of service like a personal assistant or a clerk.

Performer B enters the space and asks Performer A "What can I do for you?" Performer A should respond with three things they would like them to do that may be normal and expected. However, they should cap the list off with a surprisingly ironic request as the fourth item. Here is an example:

Example 1

Performer B: (entering) What can I do for you?

Performer A: (seated) Well Susan, I want you to order some more weight machines, two new treadmills, a dozen yoga balls and every morning when you get here I want you to put some jelly doughnuts out in the lobby.

Performer B: Here's the thing – jelly doughnuts are going to make people, y'know, fat. And that's not what we do here.

The rest of the scene is about Performer A coming up with valid reasons to put the jelly doughnuts in the lobby and Performer B trying to explain why that wouldn't be such a good idea or why they would be opposed to such a suggestion.

We want constantly to be looking for the idea that is not your first choice. Eventually, with practice, your first choice may become the most interesting one. But only after lots and lots of practice.

It's fun to point out that Performer B can exercise some control over the setting and the relationship by making it clear in the opening of the scene, such as:

Example 2

Performer B: What can I do for you, Doctor?

Performer A: Oh yes, Nurse, this is very important. I want you to get me a syringe, 20 cc's of biolithiline, a pint of 0 negative blood and have the attendant bring my car around stat!

Performer B: Wait, are you going somewhere?

Ultimately the intention is for the performers to convince one another of their point of view. This game, and others like it, will help you to see the validity of the opposite or ironic choice while helping you to practice finding the irony quickly. Now, these are not necessarily the funniest things ever written, however, they *are* unexpected. Challenge yourself to grasp for the bizarre or silly. Trust your instincts. Go there. You are not creating great drama. You are not even creating a linear story, necessarily. You are creating a comic sketch and the audience is not interested in logic. They have come to be entertained by you. And that is a lot easier to accomplish when you say and do things that they don't expect.

Warning: Be sure your ironic choice has something to do with the scene. Randomness for the sake of randomness can be confusing to your partner and signal the observer that you're trying too hard. Case in point:

Example 3

Performer B: What can I do for you?

Performer A: Yes, thank you. I would like a club sandwich, a side of fries, a cherry coke and a series of jelly fish stings on my foot.

The only good thing about that response is that it's not predictable. Otherwise, it really doesn't seem to fit. We are striving for the ability to be inventive, to be clever and quick-thinkers. We must adhere to the structure of the exercise yes, but we must also, as performers, stay one step ahead of the audience. If the audience gets there before you or they think they're as clever as you are, then my friend, you will begin to lose them. And when you lose them it will take a Herculean effort to get them back. We want to start making decisions that are surprising. When you startle the audience with your creativity you will be rewarded with adoration and laughter.

4. Role play

Very often in improvisational sketches my students seem to shy away from playing characters that are drastically dissimilar to them. The actors I see and work with regularly get distracted about adhering to the structure of the exercise or "doing it right" that the concept of injecting character traits into the scene totally eludes them. To me this is a lost opportunity to play more interesting characters and characters who don't fall into the same old mold. There are many ways to play character for those brave enough and hopefully skilled enough to attempt it.

Gender

First and foremost, you don't have to play your own gender. Audiences love it when women play men and especially when men play women. Choosing to play the opposite gender is in itself unexpected … and fun.

Voice

There are several ways to affect your voice to support character.

Tempo

Characters that talk fast can have wonderful stage energy. Make a choice and see if your character has an interesting vocal tempo. High-strung, excited and manic characters might have this quality. Characters who speak with a slower tempo can be very funny. Dim-witted characters, surfer types and Southerners might have this trait, among others.

Placement

This is simple. If you're a man playing a woman you can change your voice. If you're playing a child you can change the placement of your voice. For any number of characters you can change the placement. It offers you a wonderful challenge and if you are appearing in an evening of sketches it allows the audience to see some versatility.

Dialects

Using accents can be a dicey proposition if you're not good at them. If you need improvement then you should practice. Get a good book on doing dialects. Work at it. It can be hugely satisfying to introduce a quality accent into your characters. Audiences find it fun and it broadens the array of characters you can play. If you have no facility for dialects then don't do them. The same goes for imitations/impersonations. If you can do them, they can really tickle your audience. If you can't, it can be a little awkward. Although, one semester, I had a female student who liked to do an impression of Arnold Schwarzenegger. It was the worst impression I've ever heard and one of the funniest things I've ever seen.

Physicality

This concept is pretty clear but it never ceases to amaze me how few improvisers really connect their body to their work. They seem content to play characters who sound and move exactly like they do. It doesn't take much engage your body. You can do things to move differently that are subtle and effective. When you decide that you're going to make a physical choice just check in with who the character is and what they are trying to do.

Also, a wonderful way to bring a physical dynamic to your sketches is finding excuses to change your levels. Finding reasons to carefully stand on a box or a sturdy chair can create status or underscore particularly dramatic motivation. Conversely, allowing your character to find reasons to lower their physical stature can be successful as well. A character that sinks to the floor or even introduces the activity of lying down can completely alter the trajectory of the sketch in an astonishing way.

The real purpose of these kinds of changes is to bring an aspect of surprise to your work. Don't be shy about trying these things out. It can take a lot of trial and error to get to the place where you can comfortably make these kinds of bold choices. Though when you do invest in these kinds of creative ideas, the return can be very satisfying.

5. Build upon

Successful sketch improv is about creating scenes that draw the audience in and take them on a journey. Especially using the long form. I want to encourage you to be a co-creator in every scene. There are lots of ways to think about this. I tell my students it's like the game Jenga. You keep adding to the tower until finally, at last, it topples to the ground. In a sketch it's very similar. You want to keep adding to the scene. You take what your partner introduces and add to that until the scene swells to a climax and the audience has been satiated.

When each character consistently contributes new information the quality of the scene is elevated. In addition, it forces the performers to share in the creation of the sketch. No one actor should be driving a sketch and this technique insures that the scene is a shared proposition.

When you do build upon your partners bit make sure to stay in the present moment and try not to describe stories that happened off stage or talk about characters who aren't there. And whenever possible show, don't tell. These are not new ideas but they are super important. If you are able to incorporate all of these ideas into your scene then you have a wonderful chance to bring many unexpected qualities to the stage all at the same time.

½. Be spontaneous now

One of the hallmarks of the skilled improviser is spontaneity. Quick responses that seem rehearsed. Unflinching reactions that defy expectation. How do you get to that point in your craft? What does it take to get to that level? My answer is don't think. Or should I say don't take the time to think. I see the look of panic wash over the faces of my students from time to time and when that happens I call out: "SPEAK!" When you find yourself without any idea of what to say next, take a breath and just start talking. Your brain is incredible. If you utilize this tactic then words will start to come out of your mouth almost magically. What you say may not be funny. It may not be what you were hoping for. Heck, it may make no sense at all—just a bunch of gibberish. But, like every other technique in this chapter, if you continue to make these tools a part of your daily practice and you are diligent and thoughtful, you will improve. But you must do it. This chapter is useless to you unless you get out of your chair and do the work. Use everything you've got and practice as often as you can. You will see improvement in your characters and your content. You will notice an ease in your work absent of tension and fear. Be bold, be strange and have fun!

Acknowledgments

To my ladies, Heidi and Tess: everything I do is for you.

And to my theatre students, past and present, at the California State University–Northridge, for being my guinea pigs. It was a blast.

Bibliography

"Harold Ramis." *IMDb*. See http://www.imdb.com/name/nm0000601/.

Barry, Carolyne. "Why Improvisation Training Is a Commercial Audition Necessity." See www.backstage.com/advice-for-actors/backstage-experts/why-improvisation-training-commercial-audition-necessity.

"List of Improvisational Theatre Companies." *Wikipedia*. See http://en.wikipedia.org/wiki/List_of_improvisational_theatre_companies.

"Who Is Joey Novick, Esq?" See www.improvforlawyers.com/public_html_improvfor lawyers.com/Who_is_Joey_Novick,_Esq.html.

INDEX

When the text is within a table, the number span is in italic, e.g. behavioral gestures *92*
When the text is within a figure, the number span is in bold, e.g. Burgundy Loaf **36–42**
When the text is within a note, this is indicated by page number, 'n', note number, e.g.
    non-heroes 25, 28, 32, 38, 42-3, 44n2